# STEP-BY-STEP
# POTTERY
## AND
# CERAMICS

# STEP-BY-STEP
# POTTERY
## — AND —
# CERAMICS
## A CREATIVE GUIDE

Lorette Espi
Photography by Juan Espi

**Crescent**

CRESCENT BOOKS
New York · Avenel, New Jersey

This 1995 edition published by Crescent Books,
distributed by Random House Value Publishing, Inc.,
40 Engelhard Avenue, Avenel, New Jersey 07001.

Random House
New York ● Toronto ● London ● Sydney ● Auckland

Originally published in the UK in 1993 by
New Holland (Publishers) Ltd

A CIP catalog record for this book is available from the Library of
Congress.

ISBN 1-517-12108-5

**Editor:** Sandie Vahl
**Designer:** Janice Evans
**Design assistant:** Lellyn Creamer
**Cover designer:** Janice Evans

Phototypeset by BellSet
Reproduction by Unifoto (Pty) Ltd
Printed and bound in Malaysia by Times Offset (m) sdn Bhd

**Half-title**

LORETTE ESPI

*Wheel-thrown earthenware composite vessel, 65 cm (25.6 in) in
height, with incised decoration. A transparent glaze is used on the
inside of the piece, and it is fired to cone 02 (1120 °C: 2048 °F).*

**Frontispiece**

CHRISTOPHER GREEN

*Wine carafes, 52 cm (20.5 in) in height. These composite vessels are
made with a lightly grogged, buff stoneware clay body. The vessel
on the right is glazed with a tenmoku brown glaze and decorated
with a rutile pigment; that on the left was glazed with a pale
celadon green. The pieces are reduction fired in a wood-burning
kiln to cone 10 (1305 °C: 2381 °F).*

**Title page**

LORETTE ESPI

*Wheel-thrown stoneware bowl, 45 cm (17.7 in) in diameter. The
piece is decorated with iron and rutile pigments on a dark celadon
glaze and reduction fired. A third lustre firing is then done.*

**This page**

*From left to right, teapots by Joan Jackson, Lorette Espi, Joan
Jackson, Leora Lewis and Bruce Walford.*

**Facing page**

*From left to right, teapots by Joan Jackson, Peter Lee, Clementina
van der Walt, Joan Jackson and Lesley Bayman.*

# AUTHOR'S ACKNOWLEDGEMENTS

I would like to thank Lesley-Ann Hoets, Katherine Glenday, Leora
Lewis and Bruce Walford for allowing me to photograph their work
in progress as well as their finished pieces. Thank you also to my
teacher, Christopher Green, and Peter Lee, Riana Colquhoun, Joan
Jackson, Suzette Munnik, Hazel Anderson, Shany van de Berg,
Wiebke von Bismark, Clementina van der Walt, Lesley Bayman,
Paddy van Rensburg, Rose Miller and John Wilhelm for permission
to reproduce photographs of their work in this book. Also, a special
thanks to Diana Harvey for her contribution to the section on
the pinch pot, and to Steve Shapiro for letting us photograph
his studio (see page 32).

# CONTENTS

# PREFACE

LORETTE ESPI
*Reduction-fired stoneware decorative plate.*

The word potter invariably evokes the image of a craftsman bent over a wheel, producing vessels according to tradition, while the word ceramicist has a certain anticonformist ring to it, implying a person who bends the rules and expands the frontiers of the craft. The latter can be true in many cases where the artist uses the clay, just as she would steel, concrete or wood, for the qualities inherent in the material.

The ceramicist seems to be more preoccupied with the conceptual aspect of the piece, while the potter appears to be mostly concerned with form and function. Definitions, however, tend to only be applicable to extreme cases, and most clay artists simply get on with their work without defining it as pottery or ceramics. Whatever label we may put on their work, they use the same materials and equipment, and a commitment to their craft or art form is essential for both to produce work that is worthwhile and of a good standard.

Trying to learn the craft without the guidance of an experienced teacher is a long and frustrating process, and this book is not designed to replace a teacher for the beginner, but rather to be used with the help of one. Only a teacher can give the hands-on guidance that is so important when you are learning the basic skills, like how to prepare clay, mix a batch of glaze or load a kiln.

I think it is important that the initial inspiration that has brought a person to pottery or ceramics should be nurtured by examples of finished work by masters of the craft. The demonstrations of how they actually make a piece offer insights into the many different techniques that can be incorporated into your own style.

I am deeply indebted to Lesley-Ann Hoets, Katherine Glenday, Bruce Walford and Leora Lewis for their generosity in demonstrating their techniques. As in all other forms of art, the ceramicist never stands still. I would not have been surprised if, on visiting them a few months later, I had found them trying out new glazes, techniques and shapes.

I was very fortunate to have had my husband as a personal photographer for this project. His knowledge and love of ceramics shows in every line and detail of the pictures.

To all the people who helped me with this book, thank you.

# CHAPTER ONE

# HANDWORK

SHANY VAN DE BERG
*Hand-built form burnished with coloured slips and sawdust fired.*

The hand-building techniques that are used today are probably not very different from those that were employed thousands of years ago. It is one of the few areas in the ceramics world that has remained relatively untouched by technological progress as few or no tools are required. Those that are may include objects such as pieces of driftwood, old credit cards or smooth stones. The abilities that a potter needs to develop to make a good hand-built piece are no different today from what they were back then: a sense of form, timing and imagination, plus an intimate knowledge of clay and its firing characteristics. Even aesthetical appreciation has not changed that much; it has only broadened to encompass contemporary attitudes and sculptural forms.

Although handwork can be classified into three categories — pinching, coiling and slabbing — there are a multitude of variations in the way that these methods can be used. There are no hard and fast rules about how things should be done, but with practice and experience you will find a method that works for you and the clay and tools that you favour.

In handwork, most pieces are created by adding and joining clay at various stages of construction, which means that the sections have a different moisture content, which results in various problems during the drying and firing. A low-fired clay such as highly grogged earthenware will be kinder to the beginner as it will absorb some of the stresses that the clay body is subjected to during those critical stages. On the other hand, the lighter and finer clay bodies that may require higher temperatures are more prone to slumping, warping and cracking, but often yield more beautiful results in terms of texture and form.

Although handwork is a very spontaneous process, it is essential that you have a clear idea of the piece you want to make before you start in order to determine the size of your base, the direction of the walls, and the general construction of the piece. A few sketches of the intended work will certainly help in this respect.

Start by developing a good wedging technique, then make a simple pinch pot to practise working with clay and to prepare yourself for more ambitious projects.

# CLAY PREPARATION

Before you make a pot, you have to prepare the clay, whether it is made up in the studio or bought ready-made. This preparation involves wedging or kneading the clay to break down any lumps that may be present, expel any air bubbles, and realign the clay particles so that it has an even consistency throughout. Without this preparation, your pot might be thrown off centre because of a lump encountered in the clay when you are working on the wheel, or it could explode during firing because of the presence of an air bubble. Often an outer layer of harder clay will form on the outside of stored clay and has to be worked in with the rest.

If you are preparing the clay on a table covered with canvas, some of the moisture will be absorbed by the cloth, so the clay should be softer than required before you start wedging or kneading. The prepared clay will then be the correct consistency to work with. As you become more experienced, you will learn the correct consistency for your type of work.

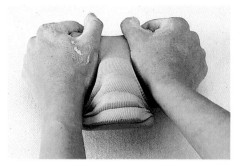

5 At least once, you must slice the piece of clay in half with a wire cutter to check the surface of the clay for air bubbles.

## Wedging

Wedging is the method that is used for preparing large lumps of clay or for the recycling of clay. Take a piece of clay and slice it in half. Leave one piece on the table, pick the other piece up in your hand and bash it into the piece on the table. Repeat this action until the clay has a smooth, creamy consistency.

Smaller lumps of clay can be wedged by breaking the clay into two pieces with your hands and then smacking the two pieces together hard enough to expel any air trapped at the joint. Continue doing this until the clay is ready to work with.

2 Cup your hands around the top of the ox head and push the clay down towards the table with the heels of your hands. At the same time, push your palms towards each other to prevent the clay from spreading outwards.

3 Note in this view of step 2 that your fingers must remain closed and in contact with the clay.

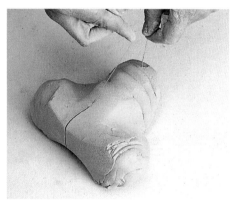

6 Here there are no air bubbles, so the clay is ready to work with.

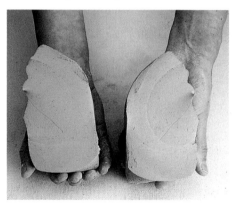

7 If there are air bubbles on the surface, slam the two pieces of clay together and knead again.

## Kneading

Kneading is the method that is most often used for preparing small and medium-sized lumps of clay. While you are kneading the clay, you should be careful not to lock any air into the folds.

1 The ox head is one shape resulting from kneading the clay.

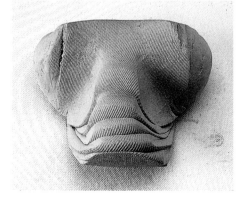

4 Push the head down and, at the same time, away from your body in a rocking motion until the nose points upwards. Use the full weight of your body and not only the strength of your arms. With your fingers, roll the ox head back into its nose, and repeat step 2. Continue kneading the clay in this way.

## Spiral wedging

Spiral wedging is a Japanese technique that is usually used for preparing large pieces of clay which are then thrown on the wheel, as this method of wedging rearranges the clay particles into a spiral alignment.

1 The shell-like shape is the result of spiral wedging.

2 Hold one section of the clay with one hand above the other.

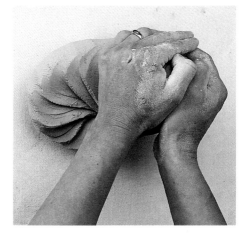

3 Apply downward pressure with your top hand while you twist and lift the clay with your other hand. Repeat until the clay is the right consistency to work with.

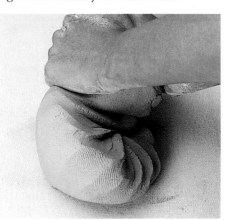

# THE PINCH POT

Pinching is the most direct method of creating a pot. Relatively few tools, if any, are required, which makes it an excellent technique for developing the tactile sense. The more refined your touch becomes, the better the pot will turn out. The experience you gain from making the pinch pot is applicable to any other pot-making technique, be it on the wheel or by hand, which is why pinching should be the first technique that you practise.

Any type of clay is suitable for this pot, so what you use will depend on what you want the finished piece to look like. Here a white stoneware clay was used to give a smooth, clean finish.

*The development of the pot is shown here. The shape is established at the beginning and the base and the walls are progressively thinned as the pot grows.*

1 Take a piece of prepared clay that is large enough to fit comfortably in the palm of your hand and form it into a ball. Press your one thumb gently into the middle of the ball of clay, deep enough so that the base of the pot will be the same thickness as the walls (an even thickness of clay all the way round).

2 Pinch the clay gently between your thumb and fingers, starting from the centre, while you rotate the pot in your other hand. Make sure that each revolution is complete and that each row of fingerprints overlaps the one below. Use gentle, even pressure, because if you press the clay too hard, you will make a deep indent that will have to be evened out at a later stage. Even pressure, complete revolutions and overlapping pinch marks are the secrets to creating a symmetrical pot.

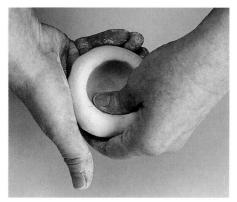

11

**3** By this stage you should have an idea of the final shape of your pot. A wide base will result in a rounded form; a narrow base will produce an elongated, closed shape.

As you work, your hands become warm and dry the clay out, which causes cracking. So, look out for signs of cracking and smooth them over with a little water.

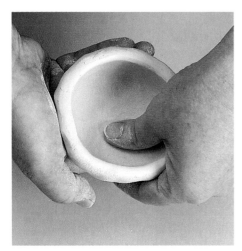

**4** As the size of the pot increases, the walls become thinner and are more likely to collapse or sag, so turn the pot gently onto its rim and wait for the clay to harden slightly. It is more economical to be in the process of making at least three pots at the same time so that you can work on the one while the others are drying.

**5** Once the clay is firm enough to enable the wall to be thinned further, the final shape can be given to the pot. Check that the pot stands properly. If it doesn't, a slight flattening of the base with sandpaper or a rasp will prevent it from rocking.

**6** The finish of the pot will depend on the type of clay you use. The grogged red earthenwares will lend themselves to a rougher and more textured finish, while pots made with the finer clays are smoother and more delicate. Here the shape of the pot is refined by scraping the walls with a thin metal kidney.

**7** Burnish the pot with a rubber kidney to smooth it, and to seal the surface of the clay.

**8** The materials and techniques that you use to decorate the finished pot will depend on the type of clay you have used and what you want the finished pot to look like. This pot was decorated with black underglaze that was applied to the clay with a Japanese brush when it was bone dry. It was then fired to cone 9 (1280 °C; 2336 °F). The surface was left unglazed.

## DIANA HARVEY
ABOVE *Grogged black earthenware pinch pots with slip decoration painted on the rims. The pieces are unglazed and fired in an electric kiln to cone 02 (1120 °C; 2048 °F).*

RIGHT *Pinch pots, both 10 cm (3.9 in) in diameter, and 6 cm (2.4 in) and 8 cm (3.1 in) in height. The pieces are burnished and sawdust fired.*

PADDY VAN RENSBURG
ABOVE *White stoneware pinch pot decorated with commercially prepared underglaze colours. The surface is left unglazed and the piece is fired to cone 8–9 (1263 °C; 2305 °F to 1280 °C; 2336 °F).*

LEFT *Porcelain pinch pot, 15 cm in diameter, with incised decoration. A wash of lightly coloured stained slip is applied to the piece.*

**ROSE MORRIS**
*Pinch pot with figures appliqued onto the surface, 14.4 cm (5.6 in)*
*in height. The piece is Raku fired with transparent turquoise glaze.*

# THE COIL POT (RAKU FIRED)

The techniques that are used to construct this pot with a lid are suitable for making any type of coil pot. Because this pot is Raku fired, it is subjected to extreme temperature changes, so a grogged clay body must be used to enable the pot to withstand the shock of rapid cooling. However, not all coil pots have to be Raku fired, and Raku is also an interesting technique for wheel-thrown and other hand-built pieces. The techniques that are used for making high-fired coil pots are the same, but structurally they must be built to withstand high temperatures or they will slump, warp or crack. The shape of this pot is unsuitable for stoneware and porcelain.

A grogged earthenware clay mixed with some stoneware is used for this pot. The proportion of earthenware to stoneware does not have to be precise, as long as there is more earthenware than stoneware in the mix. The two clays are thoroughly blended together, using the spiral wedging technique. A grogged earthenware clay can also be used with success.

**3** Widen the form further by pushing the clay outwards with the heel of your one hand while you continue supporting the outside wall of the base with your other hand.

## Making the pot

**1** First make the base. Pat about 1.4 kg (about 3 lb) of prepared clay into a flat-topped conical shape. Because there are no joins in the base, there is no chance of any cracks occurring there.

**2** Work on a bat on top of a banding wheel. Support what will become the outside wall of the base with one hand and knock a shallow bowl shape into the clay with the heel of your other hand. The symmetry of the form must be established from the early stages.

**4** Continue to widen the base in the same way, maintaining the shallow bowl shape. The pressure applied must be even so that the clay is an even thickness all the way round, except for the support around the base which will be trimmed later

## LESLEY-ANN HOETS

*For Lesley-Ann the real essence of the creative process is to remain still and unthinking in order for an idea to present itself. She works on a batch of a maximum of seventeen hand-built pots at the same time, and invariably finds that the creative development of the pots is related to that of the previous batch. On the first day of work, she prepares all the bases, and then she builds the pots over a period of weeks. Initially she adds a coil per pot per day, but as the pots near completion, she works more slowly and may only work on two pots per day. Thus she establishes a rhythm in the creative process and in the production of the pots. When it comes to decoration, Lesley-Ann's experience and familiarity with the medium frees her to work intuitively and challenge the unpredictable aspects of ceramics. She mixes her colours without scales or measures, but judges from experience what the fired colour will be.*

**5** The foundation of the pot has been established, so you can now begin to lift the wall. Rhythmically pinch the clay between the fingers and thumbs of both hands, working from the bottom upwards, turning the wheel as you go along. The thicker wall requires firmer pressure.

**6** Continue lifting the wall of the base by pinching. The form should not widen too much at this stage, so push your hands towards each other while you are pinching.

**7** The firm pressure used for pinching can be clearly seen here.

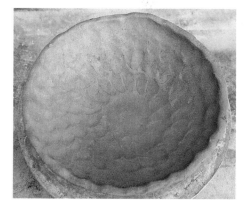

**8** Support the outside wall with your one hand and, using a curved wooden kidney, smooth the inside by pressing the clay firmly against your hand. This will also compress the wall. If the clay begins to sag, it is best to put the piece aside and wait until it has hardened enough before you continue working, or you could dry the clay with a hair dryer or blow torch (see page 69 for a demonstration of this).

**9** Pinch the rim between your thumbs and index fingers of both hands to form a thin edge.

**10** Using an onion scraper or fork, score this thin edge.

**11** To prevent stresses, which cause cracking, it is necessary to moisten the scored area with a damp sponge, and then score it again.

**12** Take a ball of clay about 0.7 kg (about 1.5 lb) in weight and make a coil by rolling the clay to and fro between your hands.

**13** The coil will lengthen as the ball is rolled out. It should not be too thin, but long enough to fit the circumference of the base.

**14** Place the coil along the scored rim of the base. Using the thumb and fingers of one hand, press the coil and the wall together.

**15** Finish off joining the coil to the base by first pushing the clay from the coil downwards onto the inside wall, and then pushing the clay from the outside wall upwards onto the coil. Pinch the coil out to match the thickness of the wall below it. Smooth the surface of the clay as described in step 8, then make and add another coil as described in steps 9–15. If you want to make a bigger pot, you must add more coils.

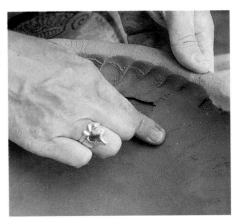

**16** The diameter of the pot is now at its widest point. Take the rim of the pot between the thumb and fingers of one hand and bend the top of the wall inwards. The amount to bend inwards depends on how high you want the base of your pot to be: for a high base, turn over less; for a short base, turn over more.

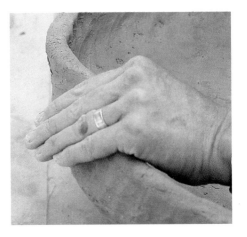

**17** Take the bent-over portion of the wall between the thumbs and fingers of your hands. Push your hands towards each other to prevent the wall from extending outwards as you pinch the clay to smooth out wrinkles, thin the walls and narrow the diameter of the pot.

**18** Using a wooden paddle, gently pat the clay to smooth the outside of the turned-over wall while supporting the inside wall with your other hand. If the clay is too soft at this stage, it will sag, so you may have to leave it to harden for a while before smoothing it.

**19** Smooth the surface further with an old credit card. This is also the beginning of the polishing or burnishing process.

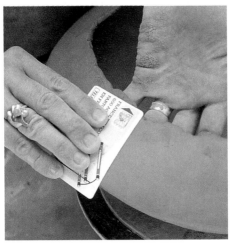

**20** Using less clay, add another coil (see steps 9–15). The coil is joined against the outside wall so push the clay from the coil down onto the outside wall and the clay from the inside wall up onto the coil.

**21** Pinch the coil out between the thumbs and fingers of both hands until the thickness matches that of the wall below it.

**22** If the clay is hard enough, paddle the pot as described in step 18 to smooth the outside wall.

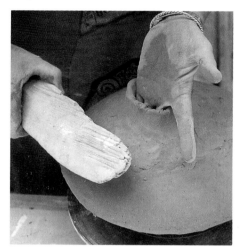

**23** Pinch the clay upwards between the thumbs and forefingers of both hands to form a neck. Always make sure while you are working that the symmetry of the pot is maintained.

**24** Pinch the neck closed with your fingers to seal the pot, and pinch off the excess clay.

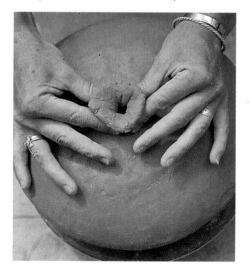

**25** Trim away the clay at the base of the pot with a potter's knife.

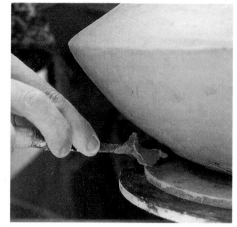

**26** When the clay is dry enough, use a wooden paddle to gently tap the top of the pot to define the shape of the pot and smooth the clay. When you are using a paddle, it is better to tap the clay many times gently than to smack it hard once.

**27** Lesley-Ann rasps the bottom half of the pot to define the shape and to texture the clay. The angle at the middle of the pot, where the diameter of the pot is greatest, is also defined by rasping.

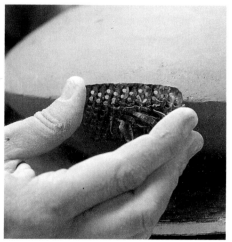

**28** Using the back of a teaspoon, mark the shape of the lid on top of the pot. The shape of the lid will depend on the design you have chosen for your pot.

**29** Following the design of the lid shown here, the pot naturally divides into thirds, so Lesley-Ann pinches up delicate lines of clay on the top half of the pot to mark these three equal divisions. She does not measure the divisions, but judges by eye where the lines should be.

**30** Using about 145 g (about 5 oz) of clay, pinch a small bowl shape with a very clearly defined rim. This will be used to make a socket for the hinge.

**31** Cut the small bowl shape in half with a potter's knife.

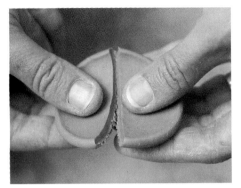

**32** Attach these two halves to the pot (opposite the pointed end of the lid here) so that the rims are facing each other at an angle. Make another small pinch bowl, halve it (see steps 30–1) and attach one half to the end of the lid (rim to the outside) that is opposite to the sockets (the pointed end here) to facilitate opening. The lines of these additions flow with the lines of the pot and form part of the decoration.

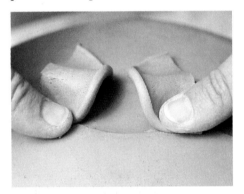

**33** Cut the lid from the body of the pot with a potter's knife. The sharper and narrower the blade, the cleaner the cut will be.

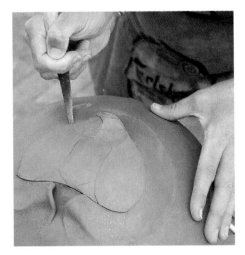

**34** Lift the lid from the body with the aid of a potter's knife.

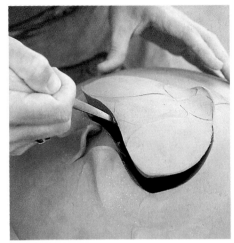

**35** Clean and smooth the inside surface of the lid by scraping it with a curved turning tool. Take care not to change the shape of the lid while you are doing this.

**36** Trim the inside of the rim of the pot so that it is of even thickness. Be careful not to change the shape or size of the opening or the lid will not fit snugly.

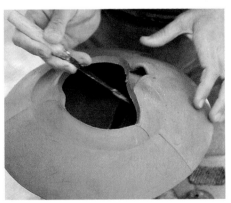

**37** Make a small T-shaped hinge with a piece of clay. This will be attached to the lid and fit into the sockets that you have attached to the pot, so check that the hinge is the correct size.

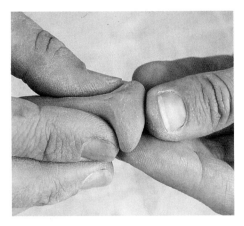

**38** Replace the lid. Put the crossbar of the hinge into the sockets. Attach the upright part of the hinge to the lid, and smooth it with your fingers.

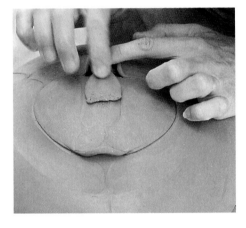

**39** A view of the hinge once it has been attached. It forms part of the decoration.

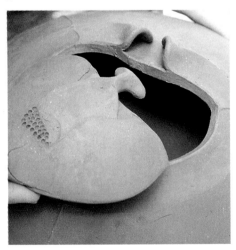

**40** Rasp the bottom section of the pot again to adjust the weight of the pot (the weight should be evenly distributed throughout the pot). The textured surface of this part of the pot remains unglazed and is a feature of the finished pot.

**41** Decorate the lid and the top half of the pot by drawing lines using the point of a sharp knife. Here, the lines spontaneously flow with the shape of the pot, and the decoration as a whole is a harmonious interaction between lined, textured and blank areas. Use Lesley-Ann's decorative techniques and design as an inspiration to create your own unique design. Cover the pot with a loose piece of plastic and leave it to dry slowly.

## Decorating, glazing and firing the pot

The green used on this pot was made by adding copper carbonate or oxide to a finely sieved white porcelain slip. A little was mixed in at a time until the shade of green was satisfactory. Lesley-Ann prefers muted colours, so she added a pinch each of cobalt oxide and manganese dioxide to dull the brightness of the copper green. The slip was sieved through a clean tea strainer.

Some of the green slip was poured off into another container and more cobalt oxide was added to make a blue slip, which was sieved through a clean tea strainer. As little as 0.1% cobalt is needed for a blue colour.

The slip is painted onto the leatherhard pot, and a second layer applied when the pot is drier. The thickness of the glaze and the temperature reached in the firing affects the colour of the finished pot.

**1** Paint the part of the design that is on the lid using slip and a Japanese brush. Here Lesley-Ann applies several layers of white slip to the petal shapes on the lid with a medium-sized Japanese brush.

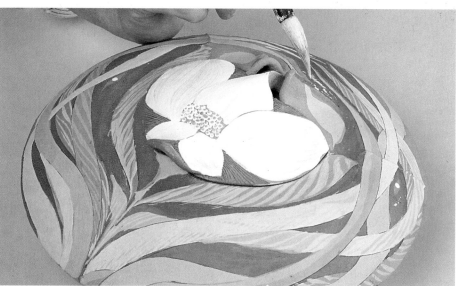

**2** She then paints the leaf forms on the body of the pot with either the green or blue slip, which is applied fairly thickly.

**3** When the painted pot is bone dry, bisque fire slowly in an electric kiln to cone 08 (955 °C; 1751 °F).

**4** Sponge off any dust from the surface of the pot with a damp sponge, and apply wax to any areas that have not been painted with slip

5 Use a thin Raku transparent glaze (see page 90 for a recipe, or buy a ready-made glaze that matches the clay you are using). Stir the glaze thoroughly. Remove the lid from the pot, and holding the pot at a tilt in one hand over a bucket, pour the glaze carefully over the pot with the other hand (here the bottom half of the pot is left unglazed). Pour glaze over the lid in the same way. Remove any glaze from the edge of the lid or the rim of the pot with a damp sponge, then replace the lid.

6 Place the pot onto a kiln shelf supported by fire bricks on the base of a Raku kiln. Place another brick between the pot and where the opening of the lid of the kiln will be.

7 The lid, which is the main body of the kiln, can now be placed onto the base. Light the gas nozzle and position it opposite the hole in the lid. The fire brick that has been placed between the pot and the opening prevents the flame from hitting the pot directly. The kiln and pot must be warmed up slowly in the early stages of the firing. Once warm, the heat can be increased until the firing is complete — when the glaze has melted and become smooth and glossy. In this case, the firing took about 25 minutes.

8 The glowing pot is ready to be removed from the kiln.

9 Lift the pot from the kiln between two metal rods and place it carefully onto damp sawdust in a shallow pit. To increase the crackle in the glaze, blow cool air onto the surface of the pot, or sprinkle water drops over the surface for a dense spiderweb crackle. Cover the pot as quickly as possible with a mixture of damp and dry sawdust. To prevent heavy smoking, the sawdust can be covered with damp sand.

10 After about 15 minutes the reduction process should be complete and the pot cool enough to handle. Remove the pot from the sawdust, dust it off, and finish it off by scouring the surface with steel wool and clean water.

11 The finished piece. The black areas on the pot were created by the smoky reduction atmosphere in the sawdust.

**LESLEY-ANN HOETS**
*Coil pot with a hinged lid. The lines of the design are waxed on top
of a dark brown base glaze, and then different colour glazes are
applied on top of this. The piece is fired in an electric kiln to
cone 9 (1280 °C; 2336 °F).*

**WIEBKE VON BISMARK**
*Hand-built stoneware bottle, 40 cm (15.7 in) in height and 40 cm
wide (15.7 in), made using the coiling method. The surface is
painted with iron slip and then burnished. The piece is biscuit fired
to cone 08 (955 ℃; 1751 ℉), and then sawdust fired.*

### RIANA COLQUHOUN

ABOVE *White earthenware coil pot, 36 cm (14.2 in) in diameter. Underglaze stain and coloured slip are painted on the pot when leatherhard. After biscuit firing, further drawing is done with glaze pencils. Transparent glaze is sprayed onto the piece, which is fired to cone 02 (1120 °C; 2048 °F).*

LEFT *White earthenware coil pot, 41 cm (16.1 in) in diameter, made in the same way as the piece above.*

# THE SLAB

The most common technique that is used to make a slab is to roll out a ball of clay with a rolling pin to form a sheet of clay (a slab) of the correct thickness. To ensure that the slab has an even thickness throughout, you can roll the clay out between two wooden dowels. Most pottery suppliers also offer a piece of equipment called a slab roller that can be used to make slabs of all sizes and thicknesses.

Slabs are used in a variety of ways. They can be textured by rolling them onto different surfaces such as fabrics, wood and lace, or leaves, grasses, stamps, shells and buttons can be pressed onto the surface once the slab has been rolled. They can be draped over moulds to make pieces of various shapes, or they can be pressed into a carved plaster of Paris slab mould to make a series of identical textured slabs which can be used to construct square or rectangular pots. (See page 85 for an example of a press-moulded, slab-constructed pot.) Tiles of various sizes can be cut from slabs, or a slab can be used as a canvas for two-dimensional ceramics — as Katherine demonstrates here.

## KATHERINE GLENDAY

*Working with porcelain is a demanding exercise. To arrive at a finished work that revels in whiteness, fineness and transparency requires dedication and patience. It isn't always possible to achieve transparency and perfectly symmetrical forms, and sometimes one quality may be sacrificed to achieve the other. There is a perpetual dynamic between technical success and creative freedom, and the challenge is not to lose sight of either.*

*Porcelain warps at the slightest provocation, and it has an alarmingly high shrinkage rate, so it is susceptible to cracking. It is strong, but rather brittle and delicate once it has been fired. It is a medium that requires painstaking wooing and it will not respond to a headlong rush into unfettered expression.*

*Katherine has concentrated on various aspects of porcelain over the years. The slab work began as an exploration of translucency and, indeed, as a means of painting on a relief canvas. Her thrown forms oscillate between celebrations of translucency, explorations of form, and canvases in the round.*

**PORCELAIN CLAY BODY**
This is the recipe for the porcelain clay body that is used for this slab. Weigh the powders and add water until a creamy consistency is obtained. Sieve the mixture through an 80-mesh sieve, and pour it onto a plaster of Paris bat. Leave it until it is firm enough to wedge.

See page 89 for the recipe for the transparent matt glaze that is used with this clay body.

| | |
|---|---|
| Serena kaolin | 11 kg |
| Blesburg feldspar | 5 kg |
| Silica | 3 kg |
| Bentonite | 1 kg |

1 Take a piece of prepared clay and flatten it out with your hands onto a clean dishcloth that has been placed on a flat surface. The amount of clay you use depends on how big you want the slab to be.

2 Cover the slab with another dishcloth and roll it out until it is about 0.5 cm (about 0.2 in) thick. The texture of the cloth will be imprinted in the clay.

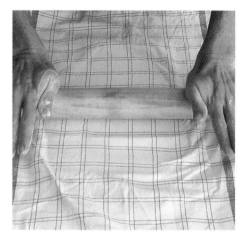

3 Remove the cloth. Using a blade cutter and set square, cut the edges to make a rectangular slab.

4 Carefully remove the cut rough edges from the slab. Wrap these offcuts in plastic and keep them to use for another piece.

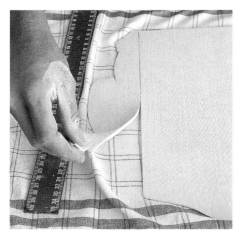

5 To create a border, cut out a rectangular piece of paper smaller than the slab and position this on the clay. First roll this gently into the clay with a wooden roller, then cover the slab with a dishcloth and roll it out again to thin it a little further.

6 Carefully peel the paper off. The texture of the clay that was covered with paper will be smooth, the area around it will be textured from the dishcloth, and a delicate edge will have been created between the border and the smooth rectangle.

7 Using another rectangular piece of paper the same size as the first, make a stencil by cutting out the negative spaces of a landscape scene. A tree and a pond are the central features of the scene here. Place the stencil on the slab, lining its edges up with the border marked by the first piece of paper. Gently rub the stencil into the clay with your fingers. Place a dishcloth over the slab and roll it gently again, using enough pressure to ensure that the slab adheres to the dishcloth, but without texturing the smooth inner rectangle. Carefully flip the slab over, peel the dishcloth off the back of the slab, then flip the slab over again (use the corners of the dishcloth to help you) and put it onto a masonite board, clay side down.

8 Peel the remaining dishcloth away from the slab. You can now draw shapes on a piece of paper, cut them out and add them to the slab by rubbing them into the clay gently, taking care not to press too heavily. Angels will be added to the sky here, and fish to the pond.

9 Use commercial underglazes, applied with Japanese brushes, to paint the picture. Here a cobalt blue is used for the pond.

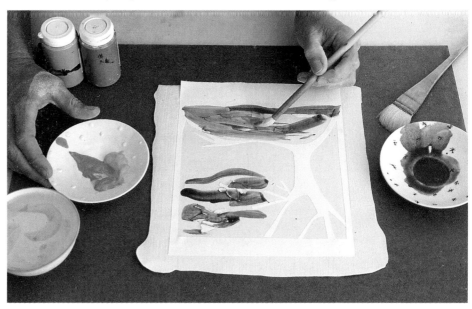

**10** Turquoise underglaze and manganese dioxide mixed with water are used for the sky.

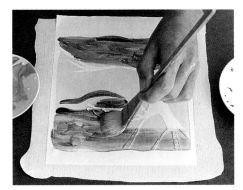

**11** The colours are painted onto the clay in varying degrees of intensity. In places the colour is diluted with water and applied like a wash. Carefully dry the excess moisture from the paint with a fan heater or hair dryer.

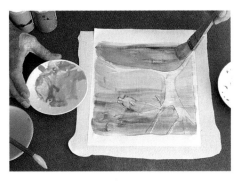

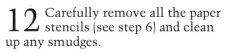

**12** Carefully remove all the paper stencils (see step 6) and clean up any smudges.

**13** Add pieces of clay to the picture to create texture and depth. Katherine uses a miniature extruder to make very delicate strings of clay. Different nozzles are used to make different shapes or thicknesses of clay.

**14** Katherine adds small pieces of the string of clay to the branches of the tree to create a relief effect, and then makes lilies for the pond by pressing small balls of clay into the palm of her hand and then pressing them into the clay. Pieces of the string of clay are used for stems. The clay is still wet enough at this stage to allow for adhesion.

**15** Clean up the edges of the slab with a blade cutter and set square, but leave some irregularity.

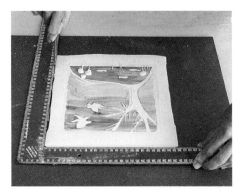

**16** Leave the slab to dry slowly. Any warping that occurs during this period is accepted as an expression of the nature of the clay. Once the piece is dry it can be slid off the masonite onto a kiln shelf. A dry slab cannot take any bending or lifting unless it is supported, so be careful. Cover the kiln shelf with a layer of alumina hydrate first to allow movement when the clay shrinks. Biscuit fire the decorated slab to cone 04 (1060 °C; 1940 °F).

**17** The hardened surface of the slab can then be drawn on with glaze pencils to create an illusion of depth or merely to emphasize form. Katherine shades various areas with black and blue underglaze pencils.

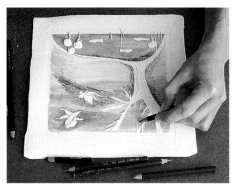

**18** Soften some of the pencil lines by smudging them with your finger. This gives a shading effect and adds tonal value to the scene.

**19** The remaining details of the picture can then be painted on with liquid underglaze that has been diluted with water to create a subtle blend of colour. Spray a thin layer of transparent matt glaze (see page 89 for a recipe) over the painted surface. Fire the piece in an electric kiln to cone 9 (1280 °C; 2336 °F).

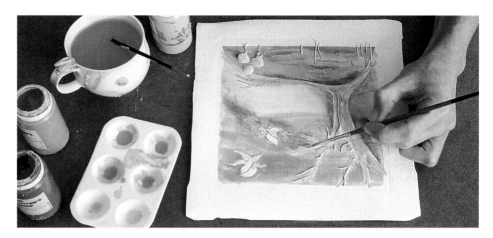

**20** The finished piece. Katherine mounts these porcelain canvases onto glass, and sometimes adds a thin wooden frame to complete the picture.

KATHERINE GLENDAY
*Detail from rolled porcelain slab, 39 cm (15.4 in) in length,*
*decorated with subtle texture and delicate additions, then*
*painted with underglaze, biscuit fired to cone 04 (1060 °C; 1940 °F),*
*and further decorated with glaze pencils. A thin layer of glaze is*
*sprayed on, and the piece is fired to cone 9 (1280 °C; 2336 °F).*

**HAZEL ANDERSON**
*Polynesian mask, 37 cm (14.6 in) in length, made by draping a slab
of lightly grogged clay over a mould, and then modelling the clay.
The piece is painted with coloured slips when leatherhard, biscuit
fired, glazed and then Raku fired.*

# CHAPTER TWO

# WHEELWORK

**LORETTE ESPI**
*Wheel-thrown earthenware bowl fired to cone 02 (1120 °C; 2048 °F).*

It is fascinating to watch a pot being made on the wheel. The way in which the clay seems to respond of its own accord to the potter's slightest movement has never failed to fascinate the observer.

The term 'throwing' may seem an odd way to describe wheelwork, but that is, in a way, what will happen to a ball of clay that is not balanced on the wheelhead — it will be thrown off by the centrifugal force that is created by the spinning of the wheel. It is this force that keeps opening the walls of the pot being thrown, and it is against this force that the potter makes the pot.

The introduction of the wheel into the studio was undoubtedly a revolution. With its help a skilled potter can produce pieces that look alike but retain their individuality at a speed unmatched by most other processes. It is a humbling sight for amateur and studio potters to see a highly trained production potter throw hundreds of items in a day, each receiving his full attention for a couple of minutes.

That is, essentially, the secret of successful wheelwork: constant repetition. Even the potter who specializes in one-off pieces should regularly throw a series of domestic-

ware items to maintain the automation of gestures that frees the mind to create any form that the imagination can conjure up.

The oldest design for a potter's wheel is a simple iron or stone disc which is turned on an axle that is almost at ground level. The pot is thrown directly on this flywheel, which the potter usually spins with the help of a stick inserted into the rim. The energy is thus stored in the flywheel so that it will continue to spin while the potter makes the pot. Either the pot is made in a single motion, or the flywheel has to be spun again.

Technological development led to new designs: the kick wheel, where the potter works in a sitting position and spins the flywheel with the feet; the treddle wheel, which is operated like an old foot-driven sewing machine; and the electric wheel, which has a range of speeds, is operated at the touch of a pedal, and is vibration-free.

Purists might say that the electric wheel has robbed the pot of some of its spontaneity, but pottery is like other arts and crafts where an 'improvement' can be seen as a trade-off of some qualities against others. You should explore all the options to be in a position to choose the equipment you will use.

## THE BASICS

Basic guidelines to wheel technique are given here, but the actual learning process is a practical one. It is best to seek guidance from a teacher, either as a pupil or as an apprentice. Whenever possible, you should attend workshops where professionals demonstrate wheel techniques so that you can learn from them. Most of all, establish a routine of practising every day. Remember that it is far more difficult to undo bad habits than to learn the correct method at the beginning.

If you follow the sequence given here and master each step before going on to the next, your progress will be quick and you will become adept at working on the wheel. Focus on learning the skills of the craft rather than on the end result — in other words, practise throwing techniques rather than trying to make a dinner service when you begin working on the wheel. Constant repetition is the secret to successful wheelwork.

### The wheel

The type of wheel that is usually available from pottery suppliers is an electric one. Kick wheels are also available (although you may have to have one made or find a second-hand one) if you do not have an electricity supply near your studio or because it somehow makes you feel nearer to your craft.

Some basic requirements that you should look for when you are purchasing a wheel are:

● a variety of speeds;
● a strong motor or flywheel that can withstand large lumps of clay;
● a smooth action — it should turn quietly and easily; and
● it must be free of rust if you are buying a second-hand wheel.

You will need a container (basin) around the wheelhead that is big enough to catch the slurry and to hold a water bowl so that you can lubricate your hands with water during throwing, and a place to put the tools and bats you will require and the prepared balls of clay. It is also important to have enough space around the wheel to rig a temporary shelf in easy reach to put finished work on.

The wheel should be cleaned after each throwing session and you should also oil it from time to time according to the manufacturer's instructions.

### Tools and equipment

The following should be at hand:

● a bowl of water,
● a sponge,
● a turning tool,
● a wire cutter,
● a sponge on a stick,
● calipers,
● a potter's needle, and
● bats.

## The clay

The clay used for wheelwork has to be well prepared. Choose clay that is not too stiff because it can present the beginner with quite a few problems. Besides being difficult to centre, it requires more skill to thin out the walls of the pot, and therefore to make them even. The top tends to be squeezed up instead of the clay being lifted from the bottom and, worst of all, you tend to use too much water, which causes weakening of the wall and cracking. So, make sure that the clay is soft and there are no lumps in it, no matter how small. It should be of a smooth and creamy consistency.

You should use only one type of clay for wheelwork while you are learning the techniques. Each clay body has its own character and will behave differently when being thrown, which will probably confuse the beginner.

## Basic forms

There seem to be an overwhelming assortment of shapes to learn when you start working on the wheel, but there are three shapes that are the basis of all forms that are made on the wheel:

● the vertical form, which is the cylinder (all vertical pots are shaped from the cylinder);
● the rounded open form, which is the bowl (many find this the easiest shape to start with); and
● the flat form, which is the plate.

The techniques for making these three forms will be described in this chapter.

## Some rules for wheelwork

● The clay must always be lubricated with water or slip. This is done by squeezing water (or slip) from a sponge and letting it run down the inside and outside walls of the pot while the wheel is slowly turning. A dry patch will cause your fingers to stick and then slip while you are pulling up the wall or shaping the pot, which will knock the pot off centre, so ensure that there are no dry patches by holding the wall very lightly between your finger and thumb and slowly sliding them up the wall from the base to the rim.

*Squeeze water or slip from a sponge and let it run down the inside and outside walls of the pot while the wheel is turning in order to keep the clay lubricated.*

● Always lean your arms against the edge of the wheel surround (basin) to steady your hands, unless a different position is specified.
● Sit up straight and keep your body weight well forward. Your nose should be in line with the centre of the wheel when you are centering, and in line with the wall of the pot when you are lifting and shaping the clay.
● The wheel must always still be spinning when you remove your hands from the clay.
● Keep your hands steady and movements smooth as any jerking or sudden movement of your hands will cause the clay to go off centre. You should take special care not to knock the clay off centre when you release it to wet your hands.
● Make sure that the wheel is turning at the correct speed for the stage you are working on (fast for centering, slower for lifting the wall and shaping) and that your hands are working at the correct speed in relation to the wheel speed, or the wall of the pot will twist and collapse.
● Remember that the outside shape follows the inside shape.

# Centering

The first step in making a pot on the wheel is learning to centre — which essentially means getting the lump of clay to spin on the same axis as the wheelhead. The method demonstrated here is just one of the many methods that can be used to centre clay.

**1** Fix a ball of clay about 1 kg in weight (about 2 lb) onto the dry wheelhead. The ball should fit comfortably in your hand.

**2** Wet your hands and cup them around the clay so that your fingers are overlapping each other and your thumbs are one on top of the other over the centre of the clay. With the wheel spinning at medium speed and your nose in line with the centre of the wheel, push the clay downwards and inwards between your hands. The little finger of one hand must be held against the base of the ball of clay to secure it to the wheelhead. Only when the clay is firmly attached, can you increase the wheel speed.

**3** Cone the clay upwards by applying pressure evenly towards the centre. Even pressure will push the clay into the centre, uneven pressure will cause the clay to go off centre. Pressing hard enough so that the clay is pushed upwards (be careful not to snap the cone), run your hands up with the growing cone. Keep your thumbs over the centre. This will ensure that the cone remains pointed. If a hollow does form at the top of the cone, it must be worked back into a point immediately, otherwise air and slurry will be locked into the hollow.

**4** To push the cone down, push it over in a slight curve with one hand, and place your other hand over the centre and start pushing downwards. Your left hand tends to be lazy, so make sure that it exerts enough pressure.

**5** Cone the clay several times. This is actually a form of kneading that realigns the clay particles, and centres the clay. Once the clay is running true and not wobbly, make a dome shape. All shapes that are made on the wheel start with a dome of centred clay.

# Securing a bat on the wheel

Many potters prefer to make their pots on top of a bat as it is far easier to lift a bat off a false wheelhead than to lift a pot off the wheel.

**1** Flatten the centred clay, pushing downwards across the centre with one hand which must be locked against your other supporting hand.

**2** Flatten the clay out further into a shallow bowl shape with your fingers. Make the centre marginally lower than the edge by applying slightly more pressure there.

**3** Watch out when an overhang, as shown in the picture, develops because if it collapses, air and water will be locked in and the edge will go off centre. So, while you are flattening and widening the clay, make sure that the base is always wider than the top.

**4** Make grooves in the clay with your index finger. These will enable a vacuum to form between the false wheelhead and the bat.

**5** Fix a dry bat onto the false wheelhead. Give a gentle bang in the middle so that the vacuum formed by the grooves secures the bat. Make sure that the bat is centred and level before you start throwing.

# THE CYLINDER (VERTICAL FORM)

The cylinder is the first shape that you should learn to make on the wheel, even though the bowl is the easiest shape to make as the walls are automatically pushed out by centrifugal force. Throwing cylinders will teach you the most about wheel technique. Therefore, although it is difficult to make a cylinder, it is important to keep trying until you get it right. This may mean throwing 100 or more cylinders, so vary the process by using different amounts of clay to make smaller and bigger forms. You can challenge yourself by setting a time limit in which to make a cylinder, or try to make a batch that are identical in height and diameter.

The cylinder is the basic form that is used to make a variety of domestic-ware items — such as coffee mugs, teacups, jugs, vases, storage jars, sugar bowls and teapots.

## Some basic rules

There are a few basic rules that you should apply when making a cylinder:

● The wall must start up at the same thickness as the base, thinning towards the top of the cylinder, then swelling out to form the rim.
● The wall can be straight or it may taper marginally from base to rim. Be careful of making the cylinder narrower in the middle or the top wider than the base as these forms are very difficult to make aesthetically pleasing.
● In order to pull the wall up straight, sit up and lean over so that your nose is in line with the rim.
● The base must be flush and squared off to the wall. If it is even a little rounded, extra weight will be carried there which can't be turned away without changing the outside shape of the cylinder.
● As you pull up the wall of the cylinder, you will find that you may tend to lean on the wall. Make sure that you are sitting up straight and that your hands are moving up the wall in a straight line and are not pulling towards you.
● Wherever possible, you should link your hands or thumbs so that they can steady each other.

## Opening the clay to form a flat base

**1** Centre about 0.5 kg (about 1 lb) of prepared clay. With your arms leaning on the edge of the wheel surround (basin) for support, cup both your hands, which must be wet, around the clay, resting your thumbs across the centre.

**2** Gently and evenly push a thumb into the centre of the clay with the wheel spinning at a fast speed. Leave a depth of 1 cm (0.4 in) of clay at the base. To measure the thickness of the clay, insert a potter's needle into the clay and slide your finger down the needle until it touches the clay. Holding your finger on that point on the needle, pull the needle out and you will be able to see what the thickness of the clay is. The base of the cylinder should be the same thickness as the finished wall at the base of the pot.

**3** To open the clay and make the floor of the cylinder, slow the wheel down, cup both hands around the clay, and push the clay away from you towards the 12 o'clock position with your thumb.

**4** The base of the cylinder has to be flat and even, so, once it is the required width, slide a thumb from the centre to the wall and back again a couple of times, or until the base is absolutely even. This action will also thin the floor a little bit more and compress the clay at the base, which helps to prevent cracking and warping, especially on wider forms. Remember that the walls and base of the cylinder should be more or less the same thickness. Gently release the clay and stop the wheel. A new hand position will be required to lift the wall.

# Lifting the wall

**1** Hold the wall at the base between the fingers and thumb of your left hand. The fingers of your right hand must be applying pressure to the outside wall, directly opposite your left hand. Holding that position, lift the wall in a continuous movement. Do not hesitate or adjust the position of your hands as this will cause unevenness.

**2** Change your hand position slightly for the next pull. The fingers of your left hand are held slightly bent against the base of the inside wall. Your middle finger will apply pressure against the wall. The fingers of your right hand are against the outside wall and resting on the bat, so the position of your outside hand will be lower than that of your inside hand. Again, you should apply pressure to the wall with your middle finger. Support the thumb of your left hand against your right hand and lift your left elbow so that it is pointing towards the ceiling. Tuck your right elbow into your rib cage to steady your arm and hand. Because your inside finger is pushing outwards and your outside finger is pushing inwards and your outside finger is below the other, a small bump will be created. Do not be in a hurry to move up the wall. Stay at the base until enough clay is gathered to lift through the wall to the rim. In this way the clay is lifted from the base evenly rather than squeezed out from somewhere half-way up the pot.

**3** The cylinder grows as the clay is lifted. Tuck the middle finger of your right hand under the bump and the middle finger of your left hand inside the bump. For shaping, ensure that your fingers are opposite each other, but here, where you are lifting the wall, your fingers must be one above the other. If you maintain this position while you pull up the wall, it will taper as it grows because the last thing to touch the clay is the middle finger on the outside wall, which pushes inwards and thus closes the shape.

**4** The cylinder will become too tall for your left thumb to be supported against your right hand, so you will have to put your whole hand inside the cylinder. It is useful to work with a wet sponge held in your right hand against the outside wall to keep the wall lubricated. Keep the same arm position as described in step 2.

5 If the cylinder is too wide, collar it by cupping both your hands around the base and applying equal pressure towards the centre. With the wheel spinning at medium speed, run your hands smoothly up the wall, closing the form inwards.

6 Pull the wall of the cylinder up once more (see step 4) to get it to the correct thickness.

7 Using a turning tool, cut away any excess clay at the base.

8 Then use the turning tool to cut an angle in at the base. This gives the impression that the cylinder has a foot and lifts the form.

9 With the wheel spinning, use a sponge on a stick to absorb any excess water from the base.

10 Holding a metal wire tautly between your hands and pressing it down on the bat with the index finger of each hand, cut the base of the cylinder free from the bat by pulling the wire towards you. Lift the bat off the wheelhead and put it aside for the cylinder to dry.

11 The finished cylinder. You need to throw at least 100 cylinders to master the technique before you can move on to making other forms. All vertical pots are shaped from this basic form.

# Shaping

Once you have mastered the technique of making a cylinder, you can then move on to learning to make different shapes. Three basic forms are shown here. A multitude of variations can be made by shifting the widest diameter of the pot (the belly of the pot) up or down. In addition, rims, necks and feet can be made in a variety of shapes and sizes and then added to the pot. For example, rims can be rounded, flattened, squared, thick or thin.

Practise making these shapes in the following order: first the round-bellied pot (right), then the high-shouldered pot (below), and thirdly the low-bellied pot (below right).

Remember that when you are shaping, your fingers must be placed directly opposite each other. Apply pressure from the inside outwards to widen the shape, and from the outside inwards to narrow the shape. Remember, too, that the walls of the cylinder must be thick enough so that the clay can be stretched into the required shape.

---

BELOW *The round-bellied pot. The widest part is across the centre of the pot.*

RIGHT *The high-shouldered pot. The widest part of the pot is above the middle.*

BELOW RIGHT *The low-bellied pot. The widest part is below the middle of the pot.*

PETER LEE
*Wheel-thrown red earthenware jar with a lid, 26 cm (10.2 in) in height. The piece is painted with cream slip and decorated with a sgraffito technique, then wood fired to cone 02 (1120 ˚C; 2048 ˚F).*

# THE BOWL (ROUNDED FORM)

Before you start, you must have a clear idea of what kind of bowl you want to make. It can only have one of two kinds of base: a flat or a rounded base. The type of base that you choose will determine what type of pot you will make. If you want the bowl to have a foot, you must use a rounded base and leave enough clay at the base to turn out a foot.

## Opening the clay to form a rounded base

1 Centre about 3 kg (about 7 lb) of prepared clay. Resting your arms on the edge of the basin for support, cup both your hands around the mound of clay and open the clay with your thumb, leaving enough clay at the base for a foot. Apply pressure at the centre of the opened clay and push the clay open further, gradually and evenly reducing the pressure as your thumb moves up to the rim. The wheel must be spinning at fast speed for this stage.

2 With your arms supported on the edge of the basin, cup your right hand around the outside wall to support your left hand, which continues to widen the wall and form a concave bowl shape.

## Lifting the wall

1 Grip the wall between the fingers and thumb of your left hand. Your fingers are on the inside wall, applying pressure at the centre, and your thumb is along the outside wall, applying pressure at the base. Your right hand supports your thumb against the outside wall and assists in lifting the clay. Slow the wheel speed slightly.

2 Holding your hands in this position, bring up a ring of clay from the base to the rim, widening the form by applying more pressure with your left hand (on the inside wall). The clay will naturally tend to move outwards.

3 Pull up a second ring of clay in the same way, making the wall higher than the required height as it will shorten when the clay is opened to the correct diameter. Always make sure that your left hand pulls up the wall starting from the centre, and support your arms either by leaning them against the basin, or by tucking them in close to your body.

4 Continue widening the form. At this stage, slow the wheel speed down and use less pressure as the form widens.

5 Gently shape the wall into a curve by applying more pressure to the inside wall at the centre with your left hand, making sure that the line inside the bowl runs true from the rim to the centre.

**6** Compress the rim. With the wheel turning slowly, hold the rim between the index finger and thumb of your left hand, while your right hand pushes a wet sponge over the rim to smooth it. The bowl can then be cut off the bat.

**7** The bowl can be left to dry until it is hard enough for a foot to be turned from the base.

**8** In this cross-section of the bowl, the area where the foot will be turned once the clay is firmer has been marked.

## Turning a foot

**1** Turn the bowl upside down onto a damp bat and centre it in the following way. Lean one arm against the edge of the basin. Point a steady finger at the 6 o'clock position so that it nearly touches the bowl. Gently give the wheel a spin with the other hand. As the bowl is turning, observe where it comes closest to your finger and stop the wheel exactly at that point. Carefully push the bowl a little in the opposite direction, towards the 12 o'clock position. Continue doing this until the bowl is centred.

**2** Hold the bowl with one hand while you fix a small coil around it on the bat with the other. This will hold the bowl securely in one position while you work on it.

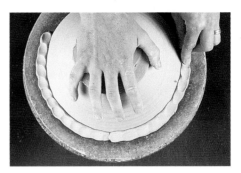

**3** With the wheel spinning at medium-fast speed, turn away the excess clay using a turning tool.

**4** The diameter of the foot depends on whether the bowl is going to be decorative or functional. The wider the foot, the more stable the pot will be. Mark the outer wall of the foot with a turning tool.

**5** Cut the clay away from the foot, bearing the inside shape of the bowl in mind (see step 10).

**6** Watching the profile of the bowl, turn the clay away until the bowl has a good line from foot to rim.

**7** Mark the inner wall of the foot with a turning tool. Do not make the foot too wide.

**8** Hollow out the inside of the foot into a dome shape so that the lowest point corresponds to the line of the bowl outside the foot.

**9** If it is necessary, level the foot and smooth off any sharp, rough edges with a turning tool.

**10** If the foot could be lifted, it would be seen that the line of the bowl is following the rounded inside shape.

**11** The completed bowl. If it feels heavy, recentre it and continue turning.

BRUCE WALFORD
*Wheel-thrown stoneware bowl, 50 cm (19.7 in). Wax-resist
technique and iron pigment decoration are used on top of a
cobalt blue glaze, and the piece is fired in a gas kiln to
cone 10 (1305 °C; 2381 °F).*

**CHRISTOPHER GREEN**
*Wheel-thrown porcelain bowl, 26.5 cm (10.4 in) in diameter. The piece is decorated using wax-resist technique and glazes are applied by the dipping, pouring and painting methods. It is reduction fired in a gas kiln to cone 10 (1305 °C; 2381 °F).*

**CHRISTOPHER GREEN**
*Wheel-thrown porcelain bowl, 30 cm (11.8 in) in diameter, that is
decorated in the same way as the piece on the facing page.*

# THE PLATE (FLAT FORM)

With this method of centering one ball of clay on top of another, which is called sectional centering, it is possible to make a plate as large as your wheel or kiln can take. The technique is an unusual but interesting one that can also be used to make a bowl or cylinder. A smaller plate can be made by using only one ball of clay.

1 With the wheel spinning at fast speed, centre as large a lump of prepared clay as you can comfortably handle — about 2.2 kg (about 5 lb). Make a shallow concave shape by applying more pressure to the centre with the fingers of your left hand and applying more gentle pressure as your hand moves outwards. Before moving on to step 2, sponge away any slurry or water from the clay and then clean and dry your hands.

2 Take a second, slightly smaller ball of clay and place it into the hollow centre of the clay on the wheel. About 1.8 kg (about 4 lb) of clay is used here. Be very careful not to trap any air or water where the two surfaces meet.

3 Cone the smaller piece of clay a couple of times to centre it.

4 Making sure that the base of the second lump is always wider than the top, push it into the clay below. Watch that no air or water are trapped between the surfaces while you are joining them.

5 Shape the clay into a dome and with the edge of one hand across the centre, push downwards so that the clay begins to spread. It must spread from the base — while it is flattening, the base is always wider than the top. A certain amount of pressure from the other hand is required to keep the top of the lump inwards to allow the spread to happen at the base.

6 When the clay becomes too wide to continue flattening it as in step 5, a different technique is required. Working with both hands together as in step 1, make a shallow, concave bowl shape.

7 With your hands opposite each other and cupped over the rim of the clay, push downwards. Again the pressure in your hands must be distributed in such a way that the clay is spreading from the base, so the pressure applied is downwards and inwards.

**8** Bring out more clay to the edge by making the hollow again for the inside of the plate. A plate may be marginally bowl-shaped or flat, but the centre must never be higher than the rim.

**9** Flatten the edges as in step 7. Don't make the base too thin, especially in the centre. Keep checking the thickness of the centre with a potter's needle.

**10** With the wheel gently spinning at medium speed, start gathering the clay at the base to pull up a wall. Do not be in a hurry to move your hands. Because it is a large plate, you must make sure that the wheel has turned a complete revolution before your hands start moving up the wall.

**11** Lift the wall of the plate as you would to make a cylinder.

**12** The height and thickness of the wall will determine the width and thickness of the eventual rim of the plate. Compress the rim.

**13** The wheel must now turn very slowly. Hold the wall between the thumb and fingers of your one hand, which is supported by the other. Mark off a point on the wall from where the rim will begin. From that point, push slowly downwards until the rim is as flat as you can make it. It does pull up again as it is drying.

**14** Compress the rim again. This does help to keep the shape round. When the clay has hardened a little, the rim can be flattened further.

**15** With a potter's needle, make a groove around the base as a guide for the cutting wire, then cut the base from the bat. It is best to cut through the base again when the plate has dried a little because it tends to stick to the bat again.

**16** The plate can now be left until it is leatherhard so that it can be turned.

## Turning the plate

**1** Turn the plate upside down and centre it onto a damp bat. Secure the plate to the bat with a thin coil of clay. Using a big turning tool, begin to slice away at the rough edge.

**2** Cut away the excess clay from the base with a turning tool while the wheel is spinning at a medium to fast speed.

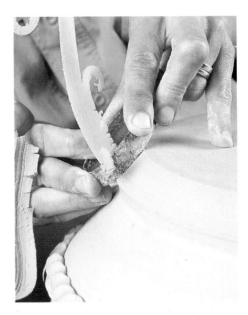

**3** Using a smaller turning tool, mark off where the footring will be and start cutting the clay away. The outside wall of the footring is angled slightly inwards.

**4** The outside shape follows the inside shape. Define where the rim and footring begin.

**5** Mark the inside wall of the footring. Note the width of the footring shown here.

**6** Mark the centre support. Sometimes a second footring will be needed here to prevent sagging.

**7** Shave the clay away between the two rings in a convex shape.

**8** Soften all the sharp edges by angling them with a turning tool.

**9** The centre support must be lower than the footring, so shave off any excess clay.

**10** The turned plate. Note the convex shape of the base, which follows the concave shape on the inside of the plate.

51

LORETTE ESPI
*Wheel-thrown white earthenware plate, 50 cm (19.7 in) in diameter. The piece is decorated with coloured slips using sponging and painting techniques. After the biscuit firing, a transparent glaze is sprayed on the piece, and it is fired in an electric kiln to cone 02 (1120 °C; 2048 °F).*

**LORETTE ESPI**
*Large, wheel-thrown stoneware plate, 50 cm (19.7 in) in diameter. The piece is decorated using the wax-resist technique over which multiple layers of glaze are painted, and then reduction fired in a wood kiln to cone 10 (1305 °C; 2381 °F).*

**LORETTE ESPI**
*Wheel-thrown white earthenware teapot,
14 cm (5.5 in) in height. The piece is
decorated with coloured slips when
leatherhard, biscuit fired and then dipped
in a transparent glaze and fired to cone 02
(1120 ˚C; 2048 ˚F) in an electric kiln.*

# THE TEAPOT

The most intriguing of all traditional forms, the teapot has irresistible appeal, even though it is the most time-consuming and uneconomic item of the domestic-ware range to make. Its appeal lies mainly in the complexity of its form, which is both a technical and an artistic challenge. Four entirely different elements must be created separately, calling for a sound grasp of most of the processes of pot-making. These elements must then be assembled into an asymmetrical but integrated whole, which must work on an aesthetic and practical level. In creating the character of the teapot you can be as experimental or as fanciful as the limits of your imagination allow, but there is one golden rule: the teapot must work. A functional teapot must feel balanced in your hand; it must lift without heaviness; it must pour without trickling, dripping or losing its lid; and it must be tough enough to withstand repeated use. So, when you design the body of the teapot, be it in a traditional or contemporary style, bear all the additions in mind. Within these restrictions there will be as many different variations as there are potters. This is abundantly evident in the rich variety of teapots that have been produced since tea drinking began.

## LORETTE ESPI

*It is a truism to say that your work as a potter will be affected by the materials you use. Somehow the plastic qualities of the clay, be it earthenware, stoneware or porcelain, will guide your hands towards chunky, delicate, utilitarian, decorative, fanciful or down-to-earth shapes. The colour of the clay and the way it reflects light through a glaze will also push you towards sombre or colourful, bold or intricate patterns in your decoration.*

*I work simultaneously with white earthenware and porcelain in an electric kiln and with stoneware in a wood-fired kiln. In the first case, I can create highly colourful and intricate patterns that will fire automatically in the electric kiln with very reliable and predictable results. In the second case, after a firing that might require feeding pieces of wood into the kiln for up to 16 hours, I might take a piece out, not recognize it at first, then say to myself: 'Hey! That is a nice piece!' For me, this duality is the essence of my craft.*

## Preparation

You must consider the design of the whole teapot before you make the individual parts, otherwise there is a risk that the teapot will not fit together properly or it will not form a coherent unit. You should also consider the medium that you will use. Many tea lovers believe that a better cup of tea is made in a brown teapot than a porcelain one. However, earthenware is weaker and more prone to chipping. Porcelain is stronger because the higher the firing temperature of the clay, the stronger the pot. From a decorative point of view, the lower the firing temperature, the wider the palette of colours at your disposal is, as many colours burn out at high temperatures. This teapot was made with white earthenware clay, which allows a broad scope for colourful decoration.

If you are using porcelain or white earthenware clay, you must make sure that every piece of equipment and all the tools the clay will come into contact with are clean. This is a laborious but essential task.

## Making the body

I never work directly onto the wheelhead but rather on top of bats. Make sure the bat you use is the right size for the pot you are making. It is pointless to use a large bat on which to make a small pot and vice versa.

1 Centre about 1 kg (2 lb) of prepared clay and then open it into a narrow bowl shape. About 2 cm (0.8 in) clay should be left at the base for a foot to be turned out of later. Check the thickness of the clay with a potter's needle.

**2** Pull up a cylinder, leaving the inside base rounded. Leave enough clay at the bottom of the outside wall for the foot.

**3** The cylinder should be pulled up 18 cm (7 in). This is higher than the finished pot will be, but the wall will shorten when the pot is being shaped. The wall must also be thick enough to allow for thinning when the belly of the pot is being shaped.

**4** Leave 2 cm (0.8 in) at the bottom of the cylinder for the foot. From just above the foot, open the clay out to form a high-shouldered pot. The widest point is well above the middle of the pot. Compress the rim.

**5** Widen the pot to the final shape. Do not repeat this stage too often as it causes the belly to go off centre and the clay to drop. After the shaping of the pot is complete, correct and compress the rim with a sponge. This will help to keep the opening round.

**6** With a sponge attached to a stick, soak up the water from the bottom of the pot. Never allow too much water to accumulate inside as it will cause cracking at the base.

**7** The diameter of the opening at the top of the pot must be measured with calipers so that the lid can be made to fit. Make sure that you hold the calipers vertical when you measure. They should just be able to go through the opening at its widest part. The measurement here is 7 cm (2.75 in).

**8** Trim the bottom of the pot with a turning tool and then cut the pot from the bat with a thin wire cutter. Carefully lift the bat off the wheel, keeping it level.

## Making the spout

The spout is the most important part of the teapot, and also the most difficult to make so, to allow for mistakes, make at least two spouts per teapot. There seem to be no rules about how to make a good spout, but here are a few pointers to help:

● To pour well, the shape must taper towards the end to ensure maximum pressure at that point. Without that pressure the liquid would spill down the wall of the spout and not be projected in a jet-like curve.
● The end of the spout should be thin to ensure a good cutting edge. It is not aesthetic to turn the lip over as you would for a jug, but at least the thin edge will ensure a clean cut in the flow of liquid, which will prevent dripping.
● There must be enough holes in the grid. Too few holes will cause clogging and trickling during pouring.
● Make sure that the inside of the spout is clean before attaching it to the teapot to avoid blockages.
● Different shaped spouts can also be made by stroking the upper part of the spout with a wet hand just after it has been made.

1 On a small bat, centre 0.22 kg (0.5 lb) of prepared clay. Open it to the bat, so that there is no base, to a width of about 8 cm (about 3 in). Pull up a cylinder that tapers sharply to a narrow top.

2 It may be necessary to collar the shape by cupping both your hands around the form and pressing inwards. Make sure that the wheel is spinning as fast as for centering while you are doing this.

3 The spout can now be narrowed further. Wet your hands and then, starting at the base, hold the clay between your index fingers and thumbs of both hands and run them up the wall of the spout, narrowing the spout as you go up. This action will also thicken the wall.

4 To thin the narrow top part of the wall, insert a potter's needle into the opening at the top, and using it as a finger, pull up the wall. Correct the shape from the outside using the same action as in step 3. If necessary, the top of the spout can be trimmed off with a potter's needle. The line of the spout must run true from base to lip. There should be no irregular bumps in it and it should never open out at the top. Cut the spout from the bat with a cutting wire and lift the bat off the wheel.

## Making the lid

The most important thing to remember when you are making the lid is that it must not fall off when the tea is being poured. To keep the lid on the teapot, a high inner wall (the collar) is made so that the centre of gravity is well back. A small lip can also be added onto the wall, which will catch against the opening of the teapot.

1 On a small bat, centre 0.22 kg (0.5 lb) of prepared clay and open it up into a shallow bowl shape. Split the rim with your finger or a wooden tool. The inner half will form a collar that will sit inside the teapot, and the outer half will form the flange that will rest on the rim of the teapot.

2 Pull the collar up a little further with your fingers. The height of the collar will determine the centre of gravity.

3 Measure the diameter of the collar with calipers and check this measurement against the diameter of the opening at the top of the pot. The diameter of the lid should be slightly less than that of the teapot to allow for the different shrinkage rates as the lid and pot dry. Make any necessary adjustments by widening or narrowing the wall of the collar. Cut the lid from the bat with a cutting wire and lift the bat off the wheel.

## Pulling a handle

1 Take a small piece of well prepared clay that fits comfortably in your hand and roll it into a coil. It is worth trying to gauge the length of the handle required. Usually it is shorter than you think. Work over a bucket of clean water as this process is messy.

2 Hold the top of the coil in your right hand. Wet your left hand, encircle the clay with it and start pulling the clay down in an even movement. It is important to move quickly on the pull and never to stop or slow down along the way. Any jerk or uneven pressure on the downward pull will cause indentations, which will make the next pull difficult. If the clay does have uneven areas, it is better to start again. Experience is needed to 'iron' out these imperfections.

3 Here the the hand position is reversed to show it from the other side. Keep pulling the clay down in a milking-like action, bearing in mind the width of the handle. Do not make the handle wider than necessary. Make sure that you keep your hand straight when you move down the handle. Check this by looking at the lines you create on the downward movement. If they twist around the handle, especially towards the bottom, you are using your hand incorrectly. Redo the pull, making sure that your hand moves straight down. The handle should be wider at the top, narrowing towards the end.

4 Change the position of your hand by flattening it across the handle. Compare the different hand positions in steps 2, 5 and here.

5 Holding your hand in this new position, apply pressure between the tip of your thumb and your fingers while your hand slides down the handle. In this way you will flatten the edge of the handle where you are exerting pressure. Pull the handle several times in this way.

To flatten the other side of the handle, reverse the position of your hands. Remember to dry your left hand and wet your right hand. Pull the handle down with your right hand as described in steps 4 and 5. A handle made in this way will look delicate because of the thin edges, but will actually be strong because of the thick middle section.

6 It is always better to make extra handles in case one breaks while you are attaching it to the body of the teapot. Put the handles down to dry on a clean piece of canvas.

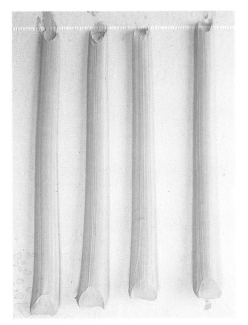

# Turning the teapot

White earthenware clay is in some ways similar to porcelain in that it has a short working period. If it is left to dry out too much before turning, the tool will hook into the clay; if it is too wet when you start turning, the clay will clog the tool and bits will stick onto the wall of the pot. There is, however, a point at which the clay is perfect for turning and you can slice the clay away cleanly with a turning tool to achieve a shape with sharp definition, clean lines and a good smooth surface for decoration. The burnished surface will also ensure a smooth glazed surface. To be able to work on the pot when the clay is just right does mean, however, that you have to keep checking it.

1 Turn the pot upside down and place it on a clean, damp bat. Don't make the bat too wet as this will damage the rim of the teapot. Centre the teapot, and then secure it to the bat with fat coils of clay. The coils of clay should support the teapot at least halfway. Using a small turning tool, narrow the base and shape the outside of the foot.

2 Cut the clay on the inside of the foot into a domed shape so that the outside shape of the pot follows the inside shape.

3 With a wider tool, trim the wall of the teapot until the line runs true to the foot.

4 With a rubber kidney, burnish the surface until it is smooth.

## Turning the lid

1 Place the lid on a damp bat right way up and centre it. Fix it to the bat with a coil of clay against the collar. Working from the middle outwards, shave the clay away with a turning tool to trim the top into a shallow dome shape that follows the inside shape.

2 Mark a decorative line a little way from the edge of the rim to enhance the dome shape.

3 Now burnish the surface of the lid with a soft rubber kidney to smooth it.

4 Score a small area at the centre of the lid and brush it with slip and ceramic glue. Attach a small ball of clay to the centre of the lid.

5 Wet your finger tips and, with the wheel spinning at medium speed, gently shape the ball of clay into a knob. Be careful not to wet the lid as that will soften the clay and cause it to collapse when pressure is applied.
  Drill a small hole in the lid next to the knob for steam to escape.

## Assembling the teapot

The body, the lid and spout should be leatherhard before you proceed with assembling the teapot.

1 The clay at the base of the spout will be slightly harder than the rest so cut that ring off. Use a cutting tool like a sharp knife so that the clay will be cut and not torn. Hold the spout against the profile of the pot and mark the curved angle of the pot on the spout. Cut that angle on the spout.

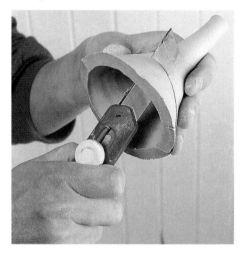

2 Thin the edges of the spout by pinching them, making it easier to attach the spout to the body.

3 Place the spout against the pot to check that the angle is correct. Hold a ruler across the opening of the pot and make sure that the tip of the spout will be above the level of the lid. The spout at this stage will be too long and will have to be trimmed later. When you are happy with the position of the spout, mark it by drawing a line with a needle on the pot around the edge of the base.

4 With a hole-maker, drill a pattern of straining holes inside the marked area on the pot.

5 Score the edge of the spout and the marked area on the pot. Apply water or slip and a little ceramic glue to each scored surface and attach the spout to the pot.

6 For this particular teapot it is important to work the spout into the line of the pot, which is done with your finger and then a sponge. As there is no grog in this clay, it is fine to use a sponge.

7 Trim the spout so that it is level with or higher than the lid. Note the angle at which the opening is cut. During the drying and firing, the spout can twist in the opposite direction to that in which the wheel spins. If it does, compensate by cutting the spout at a slight angle downwards from right to left.

8 Curving the handle into the correct shape, place it against the body of the teapot, making sure that it is opposite the spout. Mark its position on the pot with a needle. Make sure that you are satisfied with the shape and position of the handle before you attach it. It must be far enough from the body of the pot for your hand not to burn when you use the teapot. Score the area on the pot and the ends of the handle with a needle, then apply slip and ceramic glue and attach the top of the handle to the pot.

9 Attach the bottom of the handle to the pot and smooth it with your fingers. Support the handle with a suitable object while it is drying to prevent it from sagging. The assembled teapot can now be left to dry and then decorated.

# Decorating the teapot

I wait until the teapot is bone dry before I start decorating so that the underglaze can be biscuit fired onto the surface to which it has been applied. This changes the powdery chalkiness of the underglaze into a harder, porous surface which is far more suitable for the glaze to adhere to. The disadvantage of this method is that the pot is fragile and the attachments can easily be knocked off. The slightest bump could result in a chip or send shudders through the wall, causing cracks that only become apparent after the pot has been fired.

You should have an idea of what you want the finished teapot to look like before you start decorating, so it is useful to make a few sketches on paper, staying as true to the colours you want to use as possible. Underglazes fire to more or less the same colour as they are in the bottle, except for the dark blue which for some reason looks pink before firing. What will make the decoration unpredictable is the tonal value of the colours. On application they all look flat, but, where the colour has been applied thinly it may burn out altogether, and where it has been applied thickly, the colour will fire opaque and bright. In between are all the variations that will only become apparent after the firing. I use a combination of commercially prepared underglazes and coloured stains that I mix with slip made from white earthenware clay.

1 For this teapot, yellow and then green slip is applied in random strokes to the whole surface of the teapot and lid, using a sponge attached to a stick.

2 Purple slip is sponged on top of the yellow and green. The sponge is held sideways to decorate the foot and the handle.

3 Pink slip is then applied. The background is built up in this way until the whole surface is covered. Bear in mind that where the colours overlap each other a new colour will be created, for example, yellow over blue will create green. Too many colours layered on top of each other will result in a muddy brown or grey colour.

4 Paint the inside of the handle with orange slip. Use a fine sable-hair brush to paint on thin black lines to give definition to the body, lid and spout. With experience, you will learn how thickly you should apply the slip, depending on the effect you wish to create.

5 To add interest, and to break the bold painted surface, delicate black squiggles are haphazardly painted all over the teapot.

6 Small purple and black dots are also applied to the surface of the body with a brush.

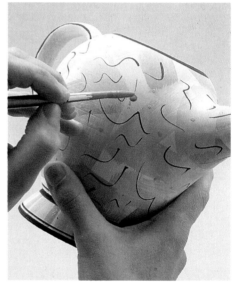

7 The decorated teapot is now ready to be biscuit fired, which is done slowly in an electric kiln to cone 08 (955 °C; 1751 °F).

# Glazing the teapot

Before glazing, I wash the pot in clean water, gently dabbing the surface. Some of the colours still smudge, even after the biscuit firing, so it is best not to rub the surface too enthusiastically. The pot can then be dried and warmed in the kiln, keeping the temperature below 50 °C (122 °F).

1 A commercial transparent glaze is used for this teapot. The glaze is well stirred by hand to mix in all the heavy sediment at the bottom of the bucket, and then, using a jug, is poured into the teapot to half fill it.

2 Some of the glaze is quickly tipped out through the spout.

3 The teapot is turned around as the rest of the glaze is poured out the top opening to ensure that the whole of the inside wall is coated in glaze. Blow down the spout to free the holes of the sieve from glaze.

4 The pot is dried and warmed in the kiln again, keeping the temperature below 50 °C (122 °F). The spout is then plugged with clay and the glaze stirred again.

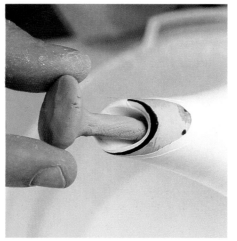

5 Holding the pot as shown, push it into the glaze with your thumbs up to the rim.

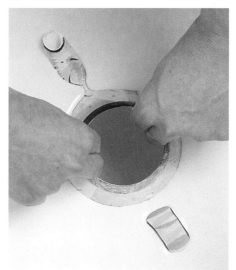

**6** The inside of the lid is waxed. The lid is then held by a pair of tongs and dipped in the glaze.

**7** I warm and dry the pot in the kiln again. Dip the rim, keeping the opening perpendicular to the glaze. The vacuum formed will stop glaze from entering the pot.

**8** The glaze must be cleaned at the foot and at the waxed part of the lid. The foot can be painted with wax before dipping, but I don't always do this as it is such a small surface to clean. The lid and pot are fired separately in an electric kiln to cone 02 (1120 °C; 2048 °F). Overfiring will cause the glaze to blister.

**9** Make sure that the kiln has cooled down completely before you open the door to take the pot out.

**LORETTE ESPI**
*Wheel-thrown white earthenware teapot,
14 cm (5.5 in) in height. The piece is painted
with coloured slips and commercial
underglazes when leatherhard, biscuit fired,
and then dipped in a transparent glaze and
fired to cone 02 (1120 °C; 2048 °F) in an
electric kiln.*

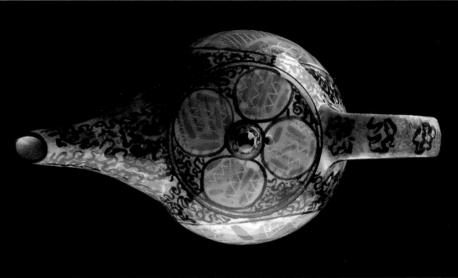

**SUZETTE MUNNIK**
*Wheel-thrown earthenware tea-set. Underglaze colour is airbrushed onto the pieces after flower and leaf additions are attached. A transparent glaze is lightly sprayed on and the pieces are fired to cone 04 (1060 °C; 1940 °F) in an electric kiln.*

**LORETTE ESPI**
*Wheel-thrown porcelain tea-set. The roses are modelled by hand and attached to the pieces after the handles are attached. They are painted with coloured slip. After the biscuit firing, the pieces are dipped into a transparent glaze and fired to cone 8–9 (1263 °C; 2305 °F to 1280 °C; 2336 °F).*

# THE LARGE COMPOSITE VESSEL

There is something seductive and satisfying about making a large vessel, and sooner or later every potter is tempted to try one. This can be tackled once your throwing ability has developed sufficiently. If you cannot centre a small lump of clay and make a pot with walls of even thickness, you will find it more difficult on a large scale. Once you start working with large lumps of clay and pulling up thicker and longer walls you will strengthen your hands and improve your technical ability too. When you have made a batch of larger vessels and you then return to making smaller pieces, the difference in control will be immediately noticeable. Depending on the shape, a large vessel can be thrown out of a single piece of clay, and, conversely, smaller vessels can be thrown in stages, using a combination of different methods. It is worthwhile to experiment and learn all these techniques. Don't be discouraged if you are neither big nor strong, as these are not prerequisites. However, you will need skill, patience and the determination to get it right. Each stage should be correct before you go on to the next or any mistake will be compounded as the pot grows until it becomes unmanageable. A good grogged clay and a strong wheel are also essential. It is futile trying to make a big pot on a wheel that grinds slowly to a halt when pressure is applied, and speeds up as the pressure is released.

## Two basic methods

A composite vessel can be made using two basic methods.

● Make the pieces and let them harden enough to support their own weight and that of the next piece to be added, while remaining soft enough to allow throwing to continue. This ensures a good line when they are joined.
● Add a coil on to a slightly hardened base and then throw it. The piece is then left to harden before the next coil is added and thrown.

## Making the vessel

1 Centre about 10 kg (22 lb) of prepared clay on a bat. If you can't centre such a large piece of clay, then use the sectional centering method described on page 48. Open the clay into a round base. The floor of the pot is bowl-shaped rather than flat as for a cylinder. To lift the clay, gather some at the base between the thumbs and fingers of both your hands and lift this ring with your hands in that position, from the bottom to the top of the pot. Repeat

this process at least two or three times, until the wall is thin enough to pull up using the technique for pulling up a cylinder. Compress and centre the rim after each pull.

2 When the required height and thickness of the wall are achieved, start shaping the form, remembering that as you open the clay the height will drop and the walls will become thinner. The shaping should be done in two or three runs up the wall.

## BRUCE WALFORD

*The tradition of good craftmanship — ranging from painting, design, restoration and woodworking to pottery — has been in the Walford family for generations. Other major influences on Bruce's work have been Shoji Hamada and Bernard Leach, both of whom Bruce perceives as having a true understanding of honesty, humility and beauty. Bruce has always set out to make good, 'honest' pots that will withstand the test of time. He sees his craft as a continual learning process — intellectually, personally and spiritually — and his greatest challenge is not to become detached from his work but to involve himself body and soul in every piece he makes.*

*Working mainly on his own for more than twenty years, he has experimented with many clays and firing processes and has personally found reduction firing the most exciting.*

3 Between the index finger and thumb of your left hand, which is steadied by the thumb of your right hand, press the rim into a point. This is called keying the rim. The first piece is complete and the bat can be lifted off the wheelhead, keeping it level while you do so. Do not cut the piece from the bat.

4 In order to prevent uneven drying and consequent warping, Bruce speeds up the drying process by using a blow torch. He dries the inside and the outside of the wall until it is firm enough to support the next piece. Keeping the torch about 30 cm (11.8 in) from the pot so that the flame is just touching the wall, he moves it up and down for 2–3 minutes while turning the wheel slowly. A lot of steam is given off.

5 To make the second part of the pot, centre about 10 kg (22 lb) of prepared clay. Open up the clay right down to the wheel, but leave the base fairly narrow because when it is turned around and joined to the first piece, that narrow base will form the neck of the vessel. The wall can then be pulled up and shaped. You should have a clear idea of what you want the completed form to look like before you start shaping.

6 Make the reverse key on the rim so that the two pieces can interlock. Turning the wheel slowly, make the key by splitting the rim with your finger or a wooden tool.

7 To make sure that the two pieces will fit together, measure their diameters with calipers. Make any necessary adjustments to the second piece if the diameters are not exactly the same. Do not cut the piece from the bat. Dry the wall of the piece (see step 4) and then lift the bat carefully off the wheel.

8 Place the first piece back on the wheel and centre it. Turn the second piece over and carefully place it on top of the first. The two rims must interlock. Cut the top piece from the bat with a cutting wire (a thin nylon wire is used here). Cutting a piece from the bat is more difficult to do when it is upside down, so make a groove with a potter's needle at the point where the wire is to cut to use as a guide.

9 Join the two pieces by pushing clay from the top piece down onto the bottom piece with your right-hand thumb. Support the inside wall with your left hand while you are doing this. Using a wooden tool and a little water, smooth the join between the two pieces together. At the same time, smooth the joint on the inside with your left hand.

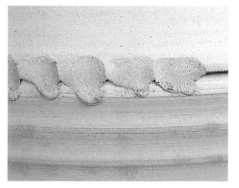

**13** Pull up a small cylinder on the neck, leaving a generous amount of clay at the top from which a wide flat rim can be formed. Never use too much water.

**14** Once the neck is tall enough, apply a downward pressure on the rim between the fingers and thumbs of both your hands to make the clay flare out into a wide flat rim.

**10** When the join is completely smoothed over, Bruce lubricates the wall from the join upwards. He prefers to use a sponge in each hand for the shaping at this stage because fingers tend to stick or slip. Never use too much water, and if drips run down the wall while you are working, dry them immediately. Note that the neck of the vessel begins to take shape.

**11** If the top is not level, then trim a piece with a wire cutter to level it and, with a swift movement, lift it off the pot.

**12** Bruce uses the coil method to make the neck and rim of the vessel. He does not score the surface before joining because both the coil and the rim are wet. Join the coil to the rim in the same way as described in step 9.

**15** To flatten and shape the rim further, put the index finger of your right hand on top of the rim. Hold the rim between the thumb and fingers of your left hand, the palm of which should slightly cover your right index finger. Support your hands by pushing your right thumb against your left hand. Any uncertain or jerky movement will throw the rim off centre.

**16** With a wooden tool or old credit card, give the final definition to the shape by sharpening the lines where they change direction.

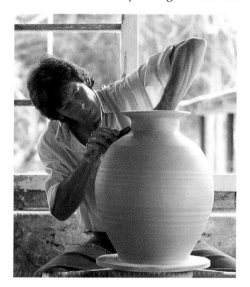

**17** With a turning tool, trim the base of the pot. This will enhance the line and give a good definition to the piece. The piece can now be cut off the bat using a nylon cutter, and the bat can be removed from the wheel.

# Glazing and decorating

**1** The pot is first biscuit fired in an electric kiln to cone 08 (955 °C; 1751 °F). Using melted candle wax, the base of the pot is waxed. The entire surface of the pot is thoroughly dusted by applying compressed air to the surface. The body of the pot is glazed with a blue glaze, using a pouring method. (The recipe for this glaze is given on page 89.) The pot is held by the neck and the glaze is poured over it, using a jug. This creates many irregularities, but adds an unpremeditated effect to the decoration, an effect which is much valued by Eastern potters.

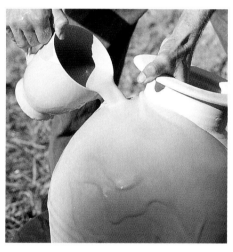

**2** A little glaze is poured into the pot and swilled round to coat the inner walls, then it is poured out.

**3** Lastly the rim and the neck are dipped. The pot must be held perpendicular to the glaze so that a vacuum is formed to prevent the glaze from running inside the pot. The pot is now ready to be decorated.

**4** A framework for the design is painted on the pot in a resist technique. Using a rubber latex, or a carpet adhesive as a cheaper alternative, Bruce bands a thin line near the base and on the shoulder of the pot with a Japanese brush. He then divides the pot into two rectangles opposite each other, separated on each side by a thin band. A contrast to the large surface area of the rectangles is created by dividing the bands into three smaller blocks. Into the middle block he applies paper resist bird and flower shapes. In the other blocks he paints a resist linear pattern with a few quick, fine strokes.

**5** He paints the whole surface of the pot, except for the rectangles, with an iron saturated khaki overglaze (the recipe is on page 89). He paints this glaze on in bold overlapping strokes using a broad flat Japanese brush.

of water first. Dampening the surface before pulling off the latex ensures a clean edge to the resist design.

8 Using a size 10 Japanese brush and a cobalt blue pigment (see page 91), Bruce paints another broad line around the inside rectangle.

6 The rubber latex is then removed. Lift a little piece with a potter's needle and spray the area with a mist

7 Remove the paper bird and flower shapes from the middle block. A second resist line (see step 4) is painted inside the rectangles and then a thin line of iron pigment.

9 He contrasts this line with a very delicate and loosely painted one. For this he uses a much finer brush and the iron pigment.

10 To decorate inside the rectangle he lays the vessel down on a folded towel. Using a flat Japanese brush and the cobalt pigment he cuts the rectangle with a broad, interesting line.

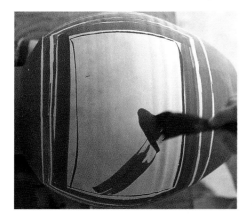

**11** He contrasts it with thin lines using the iron pigment. The decoration is reminiscent of a branch.

**12** To finish the decoration, Bruce creates two flower forms which he builds up along the cobalt line. He uses three brushes at the same time: one has been dipped in cobalt pigment, one in iron pigment and the third in a limestone, white glaze. He uses the Japanese Sumi-e brush technique for painting flower petal forms.

**13** Again the strong flower forms are contrasted with a few delicate lines painted with the iron

pigment. A pencil line can help to mark the divisions of the pot, but an intimate knowledge of the form will render this unnecessary.

**14** The finished pot is then fired to cone 10 (1305 °C; 2381 °F) in a large reduction gas kiln.

**15** The finished piece after it has been fired. Notice the change in the colours.

**BRUCE WALFORD**

*A composite vessel with a lid, 35 cm (13.8 in) in height. The piece is decorated using the wax-resist technique on top of a cobalt blue glaze. A khaki overglaze is applied, and the piece is fired in a gas kiln to cone 10 (1305 °C; 2381 °F).*

### LORETTE ESPI

*Vase, 32 cm (12.6 in) in height, wheel-thrown in two sections. A
white earthenware clay is used — 2.3 kg (5 lb) for the body and
0.9 kg (2 lb) for the neck of the vase. The second section (the neck)
is simply joined to the first section without keying the rims. A foot
is turned at the base when the clay is leatherhard. Coloured slips
and commercial underglazes are applied using paint and sponging
techniques, then the pot is biscuit fired, glazed with a transparent
glaze and fired to cone 02 (1120 °C; 2048 °F).*

# CHAPTER THREE

# SLIP CASTING

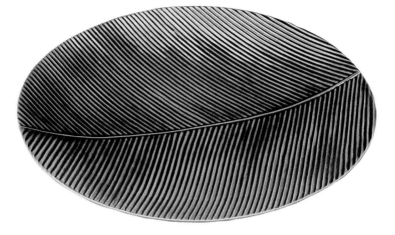

LEORA LEWIS
*Slip-cast, shallow earthenware bowl, 46 cm (18.1 in) in diameter at the widest point.*

---

**M**oulding is often regarded as more suitable for large-scale production work and it thus holds little appeal for the artist/craftsperson. Studio potters who have become drawn to the medium face a great challenge, because moulding can so easily become a lifeless and repetitive process. Yet, many have produced work of remarkable individuality and artistic flair, far removed from the commercialism of mass production.

The attitudes and perceptions of people in the world of ceramics are never static, so industrial processes have come to be viewed differently in recent years, especially as such processes can either simplify the work in the studio or expand the range of shapes, designs or textures available to the potter.

There are many different moulding techniques that are used in industry, that often require sophisticated equipment and expertise. Many of them are finding their way into the ceramics studio in a simplified form as another tool, if not an end in itself. The most relevant moulding techniques that are used by studio potters are press moulding, drape moulding and, finally, slip

casting. A block of plaster of Paris with an impression in it may be used to make identical parts, such as feet or handles, that can then be used on thrown pieces. Slabs rolled on a block of plaster of Paris that has been engraved with an intricate pattern can be used to construct a slab pot. There really are an unlimited number of uses for moulds.

Part of the studio can be easily adapted for slip casting, with only minor adjustments and a little research needed. There are many advantages to being able to use this process in the studio: it allows for quicker production; you can work on other clay projects at the same time; it is cost effective so you can spend more time on the decorative process; fewer problems are experienced during the firing as the walls can be made thinner and more even than in any other process; and forms can be altered and handworked to a point where the 'mechanistic' feel disappears, or you can take advantage of the pure clean line. Some potters use this process to produce a limited run of an article they have created. Undoubtedly, slip casting is worthwhile learning about.

# BASIC TECHNIQUES

People who are not familiar with the process of casting often ask how the pieces get such a good finish, and how they turn out hollow, so a brief explanation of the process would probably be useful.

A plaster of Paris mould is made and liquid casting slip is poured into it. The plaster draws water out of the slip and a layer of clay forms like a layer of skin on the surface of the mould, reproducing it faithfully. The longer the slip is left in the mould, the thicker the layer of clay will be as more water is drawn into the plaster. As the level of slip in the mould sinks, you will need to pour in more to top it up. When the layer of clay (the wall of the piece) is the desired thickness, the mould is turned upside down and the excess liquid slip is poured back into the bucket. The plaster continues to absorb moisture from the clay, causing the article to harden and shrink away from the mould. It is then removed and left to dry. When leatherhard, the seams are cleaned up and the piece is decorated, glazed and fired.

## Plaster of Paris

There are many brands of plaster of Paris on the market, including the kind used for making slip-casting moulds, which is available in a white powder form. It can be stored for quite a long time if it is kept in an air-tight container or in dry conditions. The powder is mixed with water. The plaster will then begin to heat up and set until it is solid. The ratio of water to plaster must be correct, as the amount of water in the mixture will determine the strength and absorbency of the mould. The best ratio of water to plaster for slip-casting moulds is 100 parts of water to 130 parts of plaster. This allows for about 5 minutes between mixing and the beginning of setting. If the proportion of plaster is higher, a denser mix is produced, which is not absorbent enough for moulds. If the proportion of plaster is lower, the mix produces a weak mould which chips and crumbles easily and is too absorbent. As a rough guide to how much plaster you will need, the quantity of powder you use will make about double the amount of plaster when mixed with water.

To mix the plaster, first measure the water and pour it into a large bucket, then measure the plaster powder and sprinkle it over the water. Islands of plaster will begin to form in the water. Let the mixture stand for about 2 minutes, then stir it by putting your hand at the bottom of the bucket, with your palm facing up, and pushing the mixture up with your fingers. This process should release any air bubbles in the mixture, so be careful that you do not do the reverse and work air into the mixture. You could also knock the side of the bucket to release air bubbles.

Continue stirring until the plaster thickens to a creamy consistency and becomes slightly warm, then pour it slowly and evenly into the mould.

Certain precautions must be taken when working with plaster. Take care that the plaster does not contaminate your clay as it will cause your pots to explode during the firing. Never pour liquid plaster down the drain as it will harden and clog it — let the plaster harden, then dispose of the solid chunks.

In the clay recycling process, dry, porous slabs of plaster of Paris are used to spread wet clay onto.

## The casting slip

Making a casting slip is not as simple as just adding water to clay powder, as too much water would have to be added to make the slip fluid enough to pour. A deflocculant, such as sodium silicate, must be used to make the mixture fluid so that more clay and less water can be used. But, all clays do not deflocculate, so a lot of testing may be required before you find a good casting slip. It is easier to buy a casting slip in powder form from a supplier and ask advice on the correct proportions of water and deflocculant to mix with the powder than to go through the long process of experimenting.

Mix the deflocculant into the water and then sprinkle the slip powder over. Stir until it is thoroughly mixed, then sieve the mixture (through an 80-mesh sieve) to remove lumps. It is best to let the slip stand for a couple of days before you use it. It can be stored indefinitely in air-tight containers, and just needs to be stirred to liven it up before use. Always keep the containers holding the slip closed when you are storing it or between pouring sessions as skin forms quickly on the surface.

Dried offcuts of slip cannot simply be thrown back into the slip bucket and re-used. They must first be dried, and then crushed into a powder, which is hardly worth the effort as recycled slip never seems to work as well as newly made slip.

LEORA LEWIS
*Slip-cast earthenware bowl, 47 cm (18.5 in) in diameter. A blue slip is stencilled onto the leatherhard clay, and the piece is bisque fired to cone 02 (1120 °C; 2048 °F). A white opaque glaze is then sprayed on and the piece is fired to cone 04 (1060 °C; 1940 °F) in an electric kiln.*

# THE TWO- AND THREE-PIECE MOULDS

Once you have successfully made a simple two-piece mould and understand the process, you can attempt a three-piece mould. Although a general rule is that the fewer the pieces you use, the better, the techniques shown here will allow you to mould practically any shape you wish. Choose the type of moulding joints that you will use and you can expand the process to five- or six-piece moulds.

Slip-casting clays are available in earthenware, stoneware and porcelain, so you can use a wide range of decorating and firing techniques. Stoneware and porcelain slips have a very high shrinkage rate, so plan the size of your piece with this in mind.

## Making a simple two-piece mould (the jug)

1 Make a clay model of the article which is going to be moulded — a jug without a handle. Here the jug was shaped from a solid block of clay. The spare adds a waste rim to the neck of the jug, which will be cut away in the clay cast. It is necessary to have this extra rim because the slip level will drop during casting as the water in the slip is absorbed by the plaster mould, creating an uneven finished edge to the piece. So, the waste rim allows you to cut the

rim of the finished piece to even it out. A line must be drawn around the clay model that accurately divides it in half. (Use a felt-tip pen so that you do not score the model.) Any inaccuracy will mean that the mould will be undercut. On an irregular shaped model such as this jug, you will have to judge by eye where the line must be drawn. As a guide, the line should be just visible when the model is viewed from either side. The profile of the jug is then cut with a sharp knife from a leatherhard slab of clay to form a template. Place the model on its side

on a bed of soft clay balls with a sheet of plastic between the model and the clay balls. The template is then arranged around the model, along the line drawn on the model. The template will also be supported by soft clay balls. Seal the join between the template and the model, if necessary, with clay and a wooden tool. Plaster does not stick to wet clay, or any smooth, non-porous surface (such as formica), when it hardens. It is therefore important that the clay model and the template are leatherhard and not dried out when casting the plaster.

## LEORA LEWIS

*While studying at art school Leora was introduced to bronze casting and was shown moulding processes for the reproduction of wax models that are used in bronze casting. At the time, she was also involved in photography and etching, so she was working with images and materials where both the positive and negative aspects had to be taken into consideration.*

*She began to focus on using clay as a medium of expression when she did a multi-media course and majored in ceramics. Clay had all the qualities she had been looking for. She found that rolled up sheets of clay can be used to take impressions from textures directly or from plaster casts. The impressed surfaces of these sheets or slabs of clay can then be rubbed with oxides or glazes as if making a frottage or monotype, or they can be scratched as if making etchings. Clay slabs or sheets can be pressed into moulds of various shapes or left flat and then cut and assembled when they are leatherhard, constructing a piece much as a carpenter or pattern-maker would.*

*Leora enjoys working on one-off pieces intuitively and not having to consider time or function. Alongside this, however, having gained experience as a model-worker in a ceramics factory, she continues to produce moulds for small runs of functional pieces, producing utility ceramics at affordable prices.*

**5** Once the plaster has heated up in the setting process, it will be hard enough to remove the wooden frame and turn the mould over. Remove the clay template (leaving the model in the mould) and make two notches in the plaster, one on each side of the neck of the jug, by drilling with a medium-sized coin.

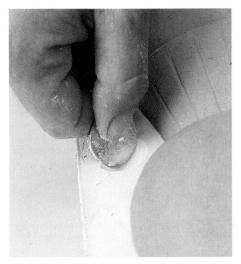

**2** Smear oil all over four pieces of wood, or make sure that they are saturated with water. Make a wooden frame with the pieces of wood, which should fit exactly around the straight sides of the template. Once the frame is assembled around the model and template, the pieces of wood should be at least 2 cm (0.8 in) above the highest point on the model.

**3** To assemble the frame, place the wooden pieces around the template and secure them with a thick elastic band that has been cut from an old inner tube, or use clamps to secure the boards. All the joints must be sealed with clay.

**4** Prepare the plaster. Wait as long as possible before pouring it into the frame because, if the plaster is too liquid, the clay model will absorb too much moisture and its shape will distort, or, if it is hollow, it will collapse. Pour enough plaster into the frame to completely cover the model and fill the box. Do not pour it directly against the model as it will spoil the release action. It is very important that no air bubbles are trapped around the model when the plaster is poured into the frame and that the plaster is properly levelled.

**6** Before you make the second piece of the mould, you must apply a sealing agent, like soft soap, to the surface of the first piece that will make contact with the newly poured plaster. This soft soap must be as liquid as water and is applied three or more times with a sponge. Squeeze the sponge dry in a towel (but do not wash it) between applications and wipe the plaster dry with the sponge before applying another coating of soap. Eventually the surface will be the colour of ivory and it will be water resistant. Because the application of soft soap makes the plaster water resistant, it must not get on to any part of the casting surface of the mould. Seal any gaps between the model and the mould with clay.

**7** Reassemble the wooden frame around the mould with the model resting in it (see step 3). Clean the mixing bucket well, then prepare the plaster and pour the second half of the mould (see step 4). Make sure that the plaster is level.

**8** When the plaster has heated up and set hard enough for it to be handled, you can remove the wooden frame. Gently rasp the plaster with a metal file to clean up the mould. It is important that the edges of the mould are cleaned up because the loose bits of plaster on the edges could crumble and contaminate the slip while you are handling the mould. Even a tiny piece of plaster in the slip can cause a blow out in the wall of the piece during firing.

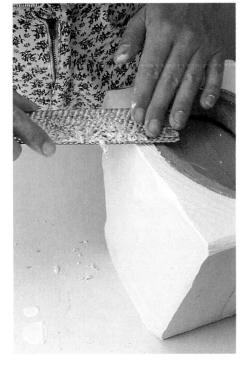

**9** Once the plaster has hardened, it is strong enough for you to separate the two halves of the mould, using a metal chisel and a hammer. Give a gentle tap with the hammer. The heat causes the plaster to 'sweat' and softens the soap, enabling the parts to separate more easily. If you do have any difficulty in separating the two pieces, wait until the plaster has cooled and use water pressure from a hose pipe to part them.

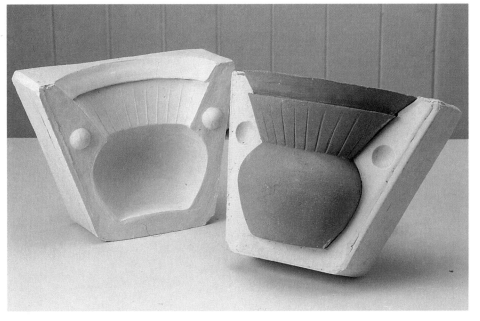

**10** The waste rims have been trimmed from these cast jugs. These pieces are bisque fired to cone 02 (1120 °C; 2048 °F) before they are glazed and fired in an electric kiln to cone 03 (1101 °C; 2014 °F). A higher bisque firing makes glaze adhesion difficult. These jugs were glazed with a black matt glaze and a semi-opaque white glaze that was airbrushed with copper carbonate for a tonal effect. The jug on the right has had a handle added to it, which was also cast in a two-piece mould.

The mould must be completely dry before you use it. This could take at least a week, but the mould will dry quicker if it is placed in a dry warm place. Do not use direct heat to try and hurry the drying process. However, it can be placed on props on top of your kiln.

The number of times that you can use the mould will vary, depending on the quality of the mould, but you should be able to use it 100 times.

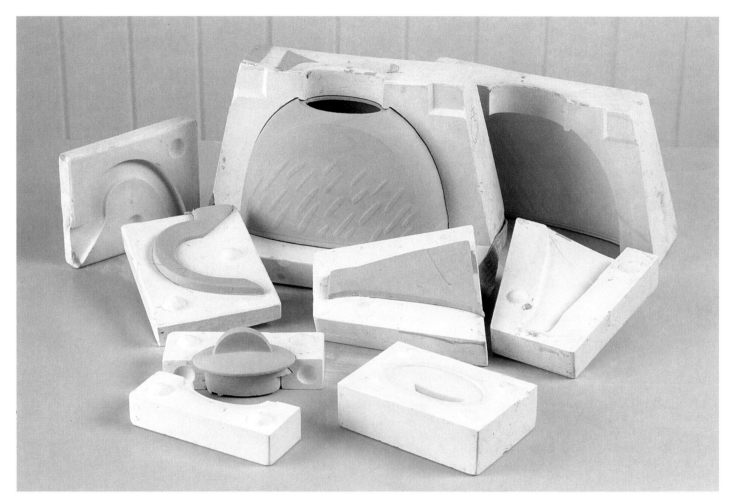

*From left to right: The first mould is a simple two-piece mould for the handle of the teapot. Note that each end of the handle is angled to match the body of the teapot to ensure a proper fit. The second mould is a three-piece mould of the body of the teapot. A detail of this mould can be seen on the facing page. The waste rim has been cut away from the last piece that is inside the mould, leaving a gulley for the lid. The third mould is a simple two-piece mould of the spout. The angle of the spout where the waste rim is attached must match the angle of the body of the teapot to ensure a good fit. The fourth mould is a three-piece mould of the lid.*

## Making a three-piece mould (the teapot)

The mould for casting the body of the teapot must have three pieces in order to obtain a concave foot at the base. The handle and spout are cast in two-piece moulds.

1 Using the same technique as for a two-piece mould, make a three-piece mould for the body of the teapot (steps 1–8, pages 79–81). A thin handle can be cast with the body of the teapot as it will become solid during the casting process. However, this handle is too thick so it must be cast in a separate mould where the slip can remain in the mould long enough to make the handle solid. The spout for this

teapot has thinner walls than the body of the teapot, so it must be cast for a shorter period of time in a separate mould. Also, if you cast the spout with the body of the teapot, you will be unable to make a strainer, which is better for pouring.

The clay model for the body of the teapot is sunk into a bed of clay in an upright position to a depth of 2 cm (0.8 in). The clay will be removed when the mould is cast for the base. A spare must be added to the rim of the teapot, and a template must be positioned around the model. Pour the first piece of the mould. The model and template must be well supported from behind or the weight of the poured plaster will distort it. Construct a wooden frame around the model and template and pour the

plaster. Once the plaster has set, you can remove the wooden frame and template. Drill notches in the mould — square registering notches have been drilled here — then apply soft soap to the plaster. Reassemble the wooden frame and pour the second piece of the mould. When it has set, remove the wooden frame and turn the mould with the model in it over (with the base of the model facing upwards). Remove the clay bed, drill notches in the base of the side walls, soft soap the plaster, and readjust the wooden frame. Pour the plaster for the final piece of the mould.

Make clay models of the spout, handle and lid of the teapot. The handle and spout are two-piece moulds (see steps 1–8, pages 79–81), the lid needs a three-piece mould.

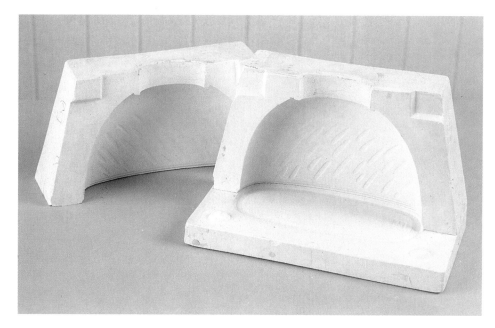

**5** Remove the spout, handle and lid from their moulds before cutting away the spare. Cut accurately along the lines of the spares to ensure that the pieces fit together well when they are joined.

**2** When the moulds are dry, assemble them and secure them with rubber bands. Pour the slip into the moulds, using a circular motion, not too far from the opening. The length of time the slip remains in the mould will depend on how thick you want the walls to be — the longer it stays in, the thicker the walls of the teapot will be. To gauge the thickness of the wall, cut into the waste rim. Add more slip, if neccessary, as the level drops.

**6** Place the spout against the body of the teapot and draw a line on the body of the teapot to mark the area. Drill several holes into that area, then score it.

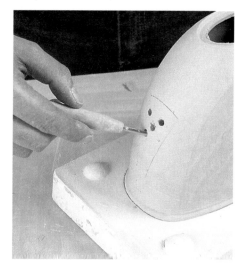

**4** The waste rim can be cut off while the teapot is still in the mould. Here the spare opening will provide a guide for the knife and a clean, accurate cut.

**7** Apply slip along the line on the teapot and on the edge of the spout that will be attached to the teapot. You could also use a good ceramic glue to aid adhesion.

**3** When the walls are the required thickness, pour out the excess slip and leave the cast to stiffen before opening the mould.

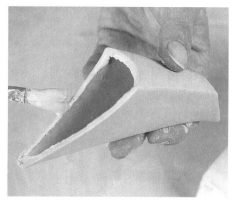

**8** Join the spout to the body of the teapot by applying pressure for a short while. Excess slip can be sponged away later.

**9** Join the handle to the body of the teapot in the same way (see steps 6–8). Put the lid on.

**10** Carefully cut away all the seams with a sharp knife, and then wipe them lightly with a damp sponge. The assembled teapot can now be left to dry, after which it will be bisque fired.

**11** These teapots were bisque fired to cone 02 (1120 °C; 2048 °F). They were then glazed inside using a transparant glaze and the pouring method, and their outside surfaces were decorated with a combination of glazes and copper carbonate and manganese dioxide that were sprayed on. They were then fired to cone 03 (1101 °C; 2014 °F) in an electric kiln.

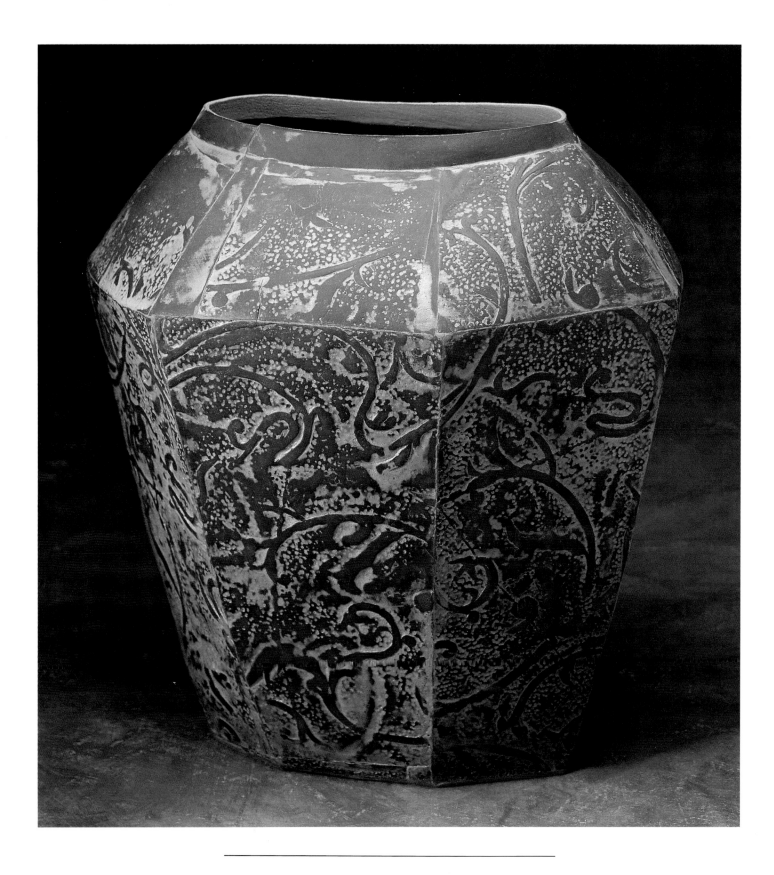

**LEORA LEWIS**
*Slab-constructed piece, 46 cm (18.1 in) in height. Slabs of clay are
pressed into textured moulds, and then joined when leatherhard.
The piece is decorated with slip and glaze and then fired in an
electric kiln to cone 03 (1101 °C; 2014 °F).*

# CHAPTER FOUR

# USEFUL INFORMATION

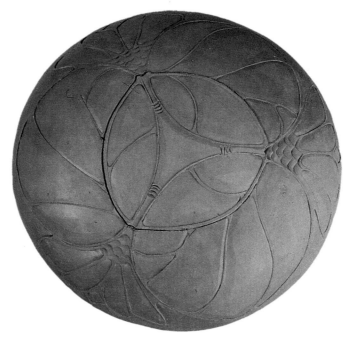

LESLEY-ANN HOETS
*Earthenware hand-built coil pot with incised decoration.*

---

There are many different ways of making and decorating a pot or a ceramic form, and this book describes a few techniques. While some potters and ceramicists may need a variety of sophisticated equipment and tools and a well kitted studio to produce the type of work they are doing, there are others, especially rural potters, who make their pots with little more than clay, which is often locally excavated, their bare hands, a few rudimentary tools, and enough wood to pack around their pots to fire them. But, most modern ceramicists or potters will need a certain amount of equipment, tools and raw materials to work with, and will find it useful and creatively stimulating to make contact with other artists or craftspeople through books and magazines, exhibitions or workshops. A studio with adequate space for a kiln and for storing and drying pots is also a necessity for most people.

Whatever route you should take in your craft, you are bound to want to mix your own glaze or slip or pigment and experiment with it at some time, and you will eventually build up your own personal collection, big or small, of tools and equipment for making and decorating pieces. You will need to know who supplies what in your area and what other services they offer, and you may wish to know which books and magazines to consult for information and as a source of inspiration. To make contact with other artists and craftspeople, you will probably want to join some sort of association that organizes exhibitions and workshops. This chapter contains a variety of general information that will be tremendously useful for those who are in the process of establishing themselves in the ceramics world, and that will also be of interest to established potters and ceramicists.

# GLAZES

A glaze adds aesthetic value to a pot, strengthens it, and for functional ware it is essential for hygienic reasons. The porous walls of unglazed earthenware will absorb liquid and particles of food, so bacteria will flourish. This will happen if patches of clay are exposed as a result of crawling or crazing of the glaze. Crazing is a sure sign that the clay body and the glaze do not 'fit' one another — they have shrunk at different rates during the cooling process.

Mixing your own glazes is not as difficult as it seems, and it is much cheaper than purchasing ready-made glazes. Also, creating your own glazes will allow you to have more control over your work, which will make it more individual. You can experiment endlessly with tone of colour, and with matt or gloss finishes.

The key to finding a successful glaze is continuous testing. There is always some space in the kiln that can be filled with small test pieces that have had different glazes applied to them in varying thicknesses. Through experimentation you can find the glaze recipe and method that best suits that particular clay body and firing temperature. This testing process in order to find the perfect finish for your work is a very exciting one as a minute alteration to the components of the glaze will be reflected in the colour and surface finish of the piece.

A more predictable method of glazing is to buy ready-made glazes. They have been developed by the manufacturers for a particular clay body that is to be fired at a particular temperature, and a palette of test pieces allows you to choose the colour glaze that you want. You can also experiment with ready-made glazes and adjust them to suit your needs.

## Basic guidelines

- Some of the ingredients that are used in glazes are toxic and so dangerous if inhaled or absorbed through the skin, so wear a dust mask and thin rubber gloves when you mix glazes.
- When you are trying a new recipe, mix only small amounts (100 g; 3.5 oz) at a time.
- Weigh each ingredient carefully. Use an accurate scale, like the triple beam scale, as you will need to be precise when you are measuring in small amounts like grams or ounces.
- Mix water into the powder until the mixture is a creamy consistency. The correct consistency is important as if the glaze is too thick, the end result will be unsightly, and glaze flaws like crazing and crawling can occur.
- Stir the glaze with your hands (or fingers for small amounts). You will soon learn by feel what the thickness of the glaze should be.
- All glazes settle, and a hard layer can form at the bottom of the container. Add 1 teaspoon of Epsom salts, diluted in hot water, or 1 part bentonite to 100 parts glaze, to keep the particles in suspension, thereby keeping the glaze soft and easier to mix.

- Push the glaze mixture through a 120-mesh sieve.
- Store the glaze in containers that can be sealed, and label test containers properly.
- Use small tiles, made of different clays, as test pieces. Make a small hole at the top of each tile so that you can hang it up on a board.
- Wipe off any loose dust from the surface of the test piece with a damp sponge before glazing.
- Using a glaze pencil or oxide, mark the name of the glaze and the type of clay (establish a system of short codes) on the back of the test piece.
- Wax the back of the test piece before glazing, and wipe off any excess glaze after the piece has been dipped.
- Double dip one half of the test piece so that you can test at which thickness the glaze works best.
- Keep a record of all your tests, and after each firing, make a note of the results next to the recipe. When you find a result that you like, test it further on a vertical surface.
- Record suitable recipes in your glaze recipe book with notes on the firing schedule, the maturing temperature, the colour and quality of the glaze, and at what thickness the glaze works best.

## Earthenware glazes

The temperature range for firing earthenware is cone 04–01 (1060 °C; 1940 °F to 1137 °C; 2079 °F). At these temperatures most earthenware clay bodies still have a measurable amount of porosity and are relatively fragile. Very little fusing occurs between the clay and the glaze. A wide spectrum of colour can be used successfully.

**Basic transparent glaze**

| | |
|---|---|
| Frit 508 | 43 g |
| High soda frit | 5 g |
| Potassium feldspar | 24 g |
| Silica | 13 g |
| Barium carbonate | 6 g |
| Ball clay 13 | 5 g |
| Zinc oxide | 4 g |

Fire to cone 04–02 (1060 °C; 1940 °F to 1120 °C; 2048 °F).

*For speckled brown, add:*

| | |
|---|---|
| Tin oxide | 6 g |
| Red iron oxide | 4 g |
| Manganese dioxide | 1 g |
| Rutile | 1 g |

*For speckled white, add:*

| | |
|---|---|
| Tin oxide | 8 g |
| Manganese dioxide | 2 g |

*For speckled blue, add:*

| | |
|---|---|
| Cobalt oxide | 5 g |
| Copper oxide | 2 g |
| Rutile | 1 g |

**Transparent glaze**

| | |
|---|---|
| Lead bisilicate | 182 g |
| Kaolin | 64 g |

This is a good glaze to use over cobalt blue slip. It has a very large firing range. Fire to cone 04–7 (1060 °C; 1940 °F to 1240 °C; 2264 °F).

*For a milky quality, add:*

| | |
|---|---|
| Tin oxide | 12 g |

**Speckled brown glaze**

| | |
|---|---|
| Super opaque glaze | 160 g |
| Leadless transparent glaze | 30 g |
| Barium carbonate | 35 g |
| Dolomite | 5 g |
| Tin oxide | 15 g |
| Red iron oxide | 13 g |
| Manganese dioxide | 4 g |
| Rutile | 6 g |

The glaze works best applied thinly. For matt, fire to cone 04–03 (1060 °C; 1940 °F to 1101 °C; 2014 °F). For gloss, fire to cone 02 (1120 °C; 2048 °F).

## Honey brown glaze

| | |
|---|---|
| Lead bisilicate | 68 g |
| Whiting | 5 g |
| Feldspar | 15 g |
| Kaolin | 12 g |
| Red iron oxide | 3–6 g |

This glaze is also beautiful over a white slip. Fire to cone 03–02 (1101 °C; 2014 °F to 1120 °C; 2048 °F).

## Bright turquoise blue glaze

| | |
|---|---|
| Standard borax frit (Ferro 3134) | 42 g |
| Colemanite or borosilicate | 22 g |
| Whiting | 7 g |
| Feldspar | 20 g |
| Bentonite | 5 g |
| Silica | 4 g |
| Copper oxide | 3 g |
| Cobalt oxide | 0.5 g |

Fire to cone 04–03 (1060 °C; 1940 °F to 1101 °C; 2014 °F).

## Matt stone white (cream white) glaze

| | |
|---|---|
| Lead bisilicate (Ferro 3498) | 50 g |
| Feldspar | 25 g |
| Whiting | 10 g |
| Kaolin | 15 g |
| Titanium dioxide | 3 g |
| Tin oxide | 8 g |

Fire to cone 03–01 (1101 °C; 2014 °F to 1137 °C; 2079 °F).

## Green glaze

| | |
|---|---|
| Standard borax frit (Ferro 3134) | 80 g |
| Zinc oxide | 10 g |
| Ball clay 13 | 10 g |
| Zirconium silicate | 1 g |
| Ilmenite | 1 g |
| Copper carbonate | 5 g |

This is a glossy opaque glaze. Fire to cone 04–03 (1060 °C; 1940 °F to 1101 °C; 2014 °F).

# High-firing stoneware and porcelain glazes

The temperature range for firing is cone 7–10 (1240 °C; 2264 °F to 1305 °C; 2381 °F). In this temperature range the clay body and glaze mature at the same time, which causes an integration between the two surfaces. This body-glaze layer adds strength and can be seen when you look at a piece of glazed pottery in cross-section. The clay becomes very hard, almost vitreous, with less than 5% porosity, making it ideal for the production of domestic ware. Unlike earthenware, pots fired to stoneware and porcelain temperatures are more prone to warping and slumping, so the shape, wall thickness and maturing temperatures must be carefully considered. The range of colours at these high temperatures is limited, but the stone-like quality of the surface is very satisfying to the eye and touch.

Porcelain is a finer white clay body of great mechanical strength which makes it possible to produce items with very thin walls. The main characteristic of porcelain is its delicacy and translucency.

Stoneware and porcelain glazes are fired in both oxidized and reduced atmospheres.

## Transparent matt glaze

| | |
|---|---|
| Feldspar | 50 g |
| Barium carbonate | 20 g |
| Kaolin | 18 g |
| Silica | 15 g |
| Whiting | 10 g |

This is the glaze that Katherine Glenday uses for the porcelain slab in Chapter 1. Fire to cone 9–10 (1280 °C; 2336 °F to 1305 °C; 2381 °F) in an oxidized atmosphere. The glaze also works for reduction firing.

## Transparent glossy glaze

| | |
|---|---|
| Feldspar | 40 g |
| Silica | 27 g |
| Whiting | 10 g |
| Dolomite | 7 g |
| Kaolin | 10 g |
| Zinc oxide | 8 g |

Fire to cone 8–10 (1263 °C; 2305 °F to 1305 °C; 2381 °F) in oxidation. The glaze also works for reduction firing.

## Blue glaze

| | |
|---|---|
| Feldspar | 184 g |
| Silica | 100 g |
| Ball clay 13 | 64 g |
| Kaolin | 70 g |

| | |
|---|---|
| Kaolin G.1 | 50 g |
| Wollastonite | 75 g |
| Dolomite | 8 g |
| Whiting Kulu II | 18 g |
| Talc | 6 g |
| Iron | 1 g |
| Cobalt | 0.8 g |
| Red clay | 2 g |
| Manganese dioxide | 3 g |

This is the glaze Bruce Walford uses for the composite vessel in Chapter 2. The glaze is suitable for reduction firing. Fire to cone 9–10 (1280 °C; 2336 °F to 1305 °C; 2381 °F).

## Khaki overglaze (iron saturated)

| | |
|---|---|
| Feldspar | 50 g |
| Silica | 20 g |
| Kaolin G.1 | 9.2 g |
| Whiting | 11.8 g |
| Talc | 6.15 g |
| Iron oxide | 12 g |
| Titanium dioxide | 2 g |

This is the overglaze that Bruce Walford uses for the composite vessel in Chapter 2. It is only used for reduction firing. Fire to cone 9–10 (1280 °C; 2336 °F to 1305 °C; 2381 °F).

## Matt limestone transparent glaze

| | |
|---|---|
| Feldspar | 33 g |
| Whiting Kulu II | 22 g |
| Kaolin | 35 g |
| Silica | 10 g |

Fire to cone 8–10 (1263 °C; 2305 °F to 1305 °C; 2381 °F). The glaze can be fired in oxidation or reduction.

*For a turquoise blue colour, add:*

| | |
|---|---|
| Copper oxide | <1 g |
| Cobalt oxide | <1 g |

## Glossy limestone transparent glaze

| | |
|---|---|
| Feldspar | 35 g |
| Silica | 35 g |
| Whiting Kulu II | 15 g |
| Kaolin | 15 g |

Fire to cone 8–10 (1263 °C; 2305 °F to 1305 °C; 2381 °F). The glaze can be fired in oxidation or reduction.

*For a lovely green celadon, add:*

| | |
|---|---|
| Red iron oxide or yellow ochre powder | 1–3 g |

Reduction fire the piece.

### Chun (blue) glaze

| | |
|---|---|
| Feldspar | 43 g |
| Silica | 30 g |
| Whiting Kulu II | 20 g |
| Kaolin | 10 g |
| Talc | 40 g |
| Colemanite | 1 g |
| Black iron oxide | 1 g |

This glaze is white if used on its own, but a beautiful blue colour if reduction fired over an iron-bearing glaze. Fire to cone 8–9 (1263 °C; 2305 °F to 1280 °C; 2336 °F).

### Tenmoku glaze

| | |
|---|---|
| Feldspar | 34 g |
| Silica | 34 g |
| Whiting Kulu II | 16 g |
| Ball clay 13 | 10 g |
| Kaolin | 6 g |
| Red iron oxide | 8 g |

This glaze is only suitable for reduction firing. Fire to cone 8–10 (1263 °C; 2305 °F to 1305 °C; 2381 °F).

### White eggshell glaze

| | |
|---|---|
| Cornish stone | 60 g |
| Kaolin | 20 g |
| Dolomite | 20 g |

This glaze can be fired in oxidation and reduction. Fire to cone 8–10 (1263 °C; 2305 °F to 1305 °C; 2381 °F).

*For a creamy colour, add:*

| | |
|---|---|
| Red iron oxide | 1 g |

### Eggshell blue glaze

| | |
|---|---|
| Barium carbonate | 27 g |
| Silica | 9 g |
| Kaolin | 9 g |
| Feldspar | 50 g |
| Dolomite | 4 g |
| Copper carbonate | 3.9 g |

This glaze only works in reduction, but it tends to jump in the kiln, causing pink flashing on nearby pots. Fire to cone 8–10 (1280 °C; 2336 °F to 1305 °C; 2381 °F).

## Raku glazes

These are low temperature glazes that are fired in simple kilns with wood, oil or gas. This method of firing originated in Japan where master potters, influenced by the Zen buddhist philosophy, used it to make vessels for the tea ceremony. Raku is valued for its spontaneous artistic qualities and the direct control the potter has over each individual piece.

Because Raku pots are fired at such low temperatures, the clay remains porous and somewhat fragile, which does make the method more suitable for the production of decorative pieces.

### White glaze no. 1

| | |
|---|---|
| Lead bisilicate | 40 g |
| High soda frit 510 | 40 g |
| Ball clay | 20 g |
| Tin oxide | 5 g |

*For green, add:*

| | |
|---|---|
| Copper carbonate | 3 g |

### White glaze no. 2

| | |
|---|---|
| High soda frit 510 (or 562) | 45 g |
| Lead bisilicate | 40 g |
| Ball clay 13 | 15 g |
| Tin oxide | 5 g |

*For turquoise green, add:*

| | |
|---|---|
| Black copper oxide | 2 g |

### Transparent glaze no. 1

| | |
|---|---|
| High soda frit 510 | 100 g |
| Ball clay 13 | 3 g |
| Bentonite | 1.5 g |

### Transparent glaze no. 2

| | |
|---|---|
| High soda frit 510 | 100 g |
| Kaolin | 4 g |
| Bentonite | 3 g |

### Transparent glaze no. 3

| | |
|---|---|
| High soda frit 510 | 80 g |
| Kaolin G.1 | 20 g |

### Transparent glaze no. 4

| | |
|---|---|
| Frit 571 or 101 or 510 | 45 g |
| Lead bisilicate | 45 g |
| Bentonite | 4 g |
| Ball clay 13 | 6 g |

### Transparent glaze no. 5

| | |
|---|---|
| High soda frit 510 | 70 g |
| Lithium carbonate | 10 g |
| Soda feldspar | 5 g |
| Clay | 15 g |

### Transparent glaze no. 6

| | |
|---|---|
| High soda frit 510 | 84 g |
| Ball clay 13 | 16 g |
| Bentonite | 1 g |

Any one of these transparent Raku glazes can be used as a base to which stains and oxides can be added to colour the glaze:

*For green or copper red, add:*

| | |
|---|---|
| Copper oxide or copper carbonate | 2–5 g |

*For light blue, add:*

| | |
|---|---|
| Cobalt carbonate | 1 g |
| Tin oxide | 3 g |

*For light turquoise blue, add:*

| | |
|---|---|
| Copper oxide | 2 g |
| Cobalt oxide | 5 g |
| Tin oxide | 4 g |

*For turquoise blue, add:*

| | |
|---|---|
| Cobalt oxide | 1 g |

*For light green, add:*

| | |
|---|---|
| Copper oxide or copper carbonate | 2–5 g |
| Tin oxide | 8 g |

*For white, add:*

| | |
|---|---|
| Tin oxide | 4 g |

*For pink, add:*

| | |
|---|---|
| Pink stain | 6 g |

*For yellow, add:*

| | |
|---|---|
| Yellow stain | 5 g |

As tin oxide is a very expensive ingredient to use, zirconium oxide can be used as a substitute.

For more variations, try adding some of the other colour stains that are available, and experiment with different colour slips underneath the transparent glazes.

Because Raku firing can be done in such a short time, many firings can be done in one session and it is thus possible to adjust the glaze in between firings. You can add small quantities of oxide to the glaze after each firing until you get the result that you want.

To know when to remove the piece from the kiln, check through the spy-hole in the kiln. When the glaze takes on a glossy appearance, you will know that it is time to remove the pieces from the kiln. Wear asbestos gloves and use long metal tongs to do so to prevent getting burnt.

# SLIPS AND PIGMENTS

Slip is always used underneath a glaze, at any firing temperature, and is applied to the pot when the clay is still wet, or at leatherhard stage. There are very few slips that can be used after biscuit firing. By adding oxides or stains to slip, you can create a palette of colour that can effectively be used underneath a transparent glaze. Use the clay body that you are working with to make up the slip if you want to be sure that the slip will work. Otherwise, experiment with some of the recipes given here.

Pigments are always used on top of a glaze, and are fired in reduction rather than oxidation. Bruce Walford's large composite vessel in Chapter 2 is a fine example of using pigments to decorate a pot.

KATHERINE GLENDAY
*Wheel-thrown porcelain bowl.*

## Basic guidelines

● To make a slip, add water to the clay or clay powder until the mixture has a creamy consistency.

● Sieve the slip mixture through a 120-mesh screen.

● If the slip flakes off your pot, try sifting it again through a 120-mesh sieve. Alternatively, try applying the slip to the pot when it is still wet rather than at the leatherhard stage.

● To mix pigments, grind the powders by hand with a mortar and pestle, and add small amounts of water until the mixture is a smooth, creamy consistency. Continue diluting the pigment until it flows easily when applied with a brush onto the glazed surface of the pot.

**Basic slip**

| | |
|---|---|
| Ball clay 13 | 50 g |
| Kaolin G.1 | 50 g |

Use this slip for earthenware, stoneware and porcelain. Sieve the slip twice. Apply it to greenware that is still fairly wet.

*For a whiter slip, add:*

| | |
|---|---|
| Zircon or tin oxide | 5 g |

*For brown, add:*

| | |
|---|---|
| Red iron oxide | 10 g |

*For blue, add:*

| | |
|---|---|
| Cobalt oxide | 2 g |

*For purple-brown, add:*

| | |
|---|---|
| Manganese oxide | 10 g |

*For green, add:*

| | |
|---|---|
| Copper oxide | 3 g |

*For yellow, add:*

| | |
|---|---|
| Vanadium | 3 g |

*For black, add:*

| | |
|---|---|
| Red iron oxide | 3 g |
| Cobalt oxide | 1 g |
| Manganese dioxide | 3 g |

**Earthenware white slip**

| | |
|---|---|
| T.R. light firing clay | 69 g |
| Kaolin G.1 | 18.5 g |
| Soda feldspar | 9 g |
| Silica | 3.5 g |

This slip works well under the earthenware transparent glaze on page 88. Fire to cone 04–7 (1060 °C; 1949 °F to 1240 °C; 2264 °F).

*For a whiter colour, add:*

| | |
|---|---|
| Zinc oxide or tin oxide | 1 g |

*For a very dark blue colour, add:*

| | |
|---|---|
| Cobalt oxide | 2 g |
| Manganese dioxide | 2 g |
| Iron oxide | 3 g |

For a lighter blue colour, reduce the amount of cobalt that you add.

**Yellow earthenware slip**

| | |
|---|---|
| Red clay powder | 200 g |
| High soda frit 510 | 30 g |
| Silica | 40 g |
| Borax | 10 g |

Fire to cone 04–01 (1060 °C; 1940 °F to 1137 °C; 2079 °F).

**Black earthenware slip**

| | |
|---|---|
| Red clay powder | 24 g |
| Ball clay 13 | 26 g |
| High soda frit | 16 g |
| Silica | 20 g |
| Black stain | ±12 g |

Fire to cone 04–01 (1060 °C; 1940 °F to 1137 °C; 2079 °F).

**Porcelain slip**

| | |
|---|---|
| English china clay | 55 g |
| Potassium feldspar | 25 g |
| Silica | 15 g |
| White bentonite | 5 g |

This can also be used as a clay body. Add any stain or oxides for colour.

**Cobalt blue pigment**

| | |
|---|---|
| Red clay powder | 92 g |
| Cobalt | 4 g |
| Manganese dioxide | 4 g |

Bruce Walford uses this pigment for the composite vessel in Chapter 2.

**Blue pigment**

| | |
|---|---|
| Red clay powder | 2 g |
| Porcelain slip | 4 g |
| Cobalt oxide | 0.25 g |
| Red iron oxide | 0.5 g |

**Red-brown pigment**

| | |
|---|---|
| Red clay powder | 12 g |
| Red iron oxide | 24 g |
| Kaolin or porcelain slip | 8 g |

**Orange pigment**

| | |
|---|---|
| Stoneware transparent glaze | 10 g |
| Red iron oxide | 15 g |
| Rutile | 5 g |

If you are not happy with the result, substitute the glaze in the recipe for another one.

# TOOLS

1. Sieve for glazes and slips. Different mesh sizes are available.
2. Glazing tongs, used to hold pots when they are being dipped into glaze or slip.
3. Bats of different sizes, on which pots are made for handwork and wheelwork.
4. Double sponge on a stick, used to sponge out excess water from the inside of pots that are being made on the wheel.
5. Natural fibre sponge, used for sponging up excess water and for decorative effects on pots.
6. Wooden ribs, used for shaping during throwing and smoothing, and for shaping the walls of hand-built pots.
7. Wire cutter, used to cut pots from the bat or wheelhead, for levelling rims, and for cutting the clay when kneading.
8. Plastic scraper, used for scoring the clay when joining sections in handwork, for combing wet slip, and for decorative effects.
9. Bamboo fluter and metal turning tool, used for cutting away surplus clay from the bases of pots being thrown on the wheel.
10. Potter's knives used for cutting and fettling, and also for grinding and mixing stains and pigments.
11. Large and small turning tools, used to shape leatherhard pots. The small one is good for turning feet at the base of small pots.
12. Handle maker, a tool used for making handles.
13. Wire loop sgraffito tool, used for incising lines in the clay and through slip.
14. Bamboo fluter for fluting the clay.
15. Atomiser — a simplified form of an airbrush.
16. Calipers for accurate measuring.
17. Slip trailer.
18. Asbestos gloves for handling hot pots and kiln shelves, and useful for Raku firing.
19. Mask to wear when mixing glazes and when cleaning the studio.
20. Japanese brushes for decorating.
21. Hole maker.
22. Potter's needle, used for popping air bubbles, levelling rims, measuring the thickness of a base or wall.
23. Flexible metal, rubber and plastic kidneys, used for scraping, smoothing and shaping.

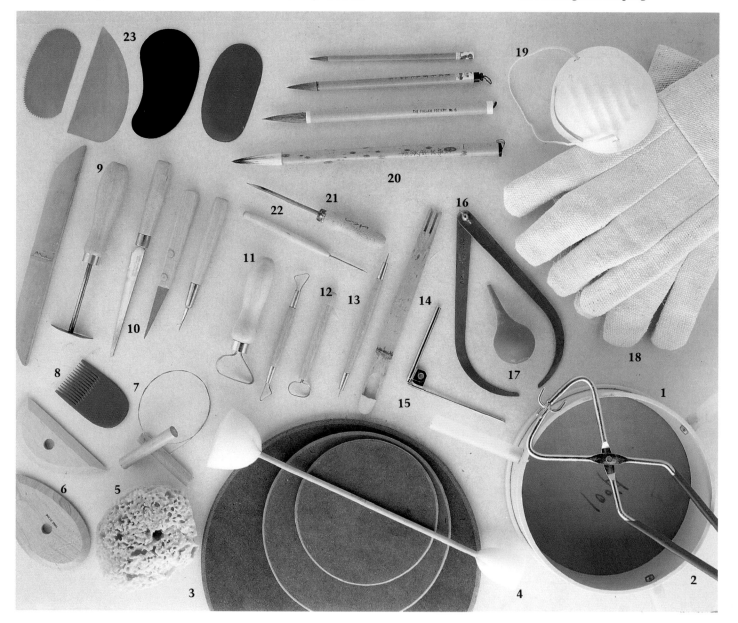

# SUPPLIERS OF EQUIPMENT AND MATERIALS

Most suppliers of pottery and ceramic materials, tools, and equipment issue comprehensive catalogs, listing their full product range. Many also stock a range of books, including imports. Most of the suppliers listed below carry a full range of equipment and materials and are willing to answer any queries that you may have. All offer a mail-order service and welcome inquiries by mail, fax, or telephone. For additional help and support, the on-line computer information services, such as Internet, America Online, eWorld, and Compuserve operate crafts forums.

---

*A & C Distributors*
PO Box 70228
San Diego, CA 92167
800/995-9946
619/222-9946
With their new product, patina and antique finishes may be achieved on any ceramic surface, including, but not limited to bisque, terracotta, porcelain and glazed finishes) by first applying *Liquid Copper Coating* followed by their ready-made patina and antique solutions. These are available in green, blue, black, burgundy, and rust. Other Liquid Coatings available include brass, gold, and pewter. All are non-firing finishes. Call or write for free brochure.

*American Art Clay Company, Inc*
4717 West 16 Street
Indianapolis, IN 46222
800/374-1600
317/244-6871
Fax: 317/248-9300
Since 1919, manufacturers of equipment and supplies for pottery, ceramics, enamelling, and crafts. AMACO™ kilns, clays, glazes, and modelling materials; Excel™ kilns; Reward™ molds, glazes, brushes, and tools. Call or write for free catalog.

*A.R.T. Studio Clay Company*
1555 Louis Avenue
Elk Grove Village, IL 60007
800/323-0212
708/593-6060
Fax: 708/593-0785
Over 20 years supplying clays, glazes, kilns, wheels, and complete ceramic supplies to artists, studios, potters, and schools nationwide. Manufacturer of Alpine kilns, the standard in gas and electric kilns for studios and schools. Call or write for 240-page catalog available for $5 including a $4 coupon toward first order, or write for a free catalog.

*Bailey Pottery Equipment & Supply*
62 Tenbroek Avenue
Kingston, NY 12401

800/431-6067
914/339-3721
Fax: 914/339-5530
Bailey designs slab rollers, extruders, electric kilns and gas kilns. 192-page free catalog.

*Bluebird Manufacturing, Inc.*
PO Box 2307
Ft. Collins, CO 80522-2307
303/484-3243
Fax: 303/493-1408
Manufacturers of clay processing equipment since 1969, Bluebird added the Soldner-designed potter's wheel to its product line in 1988. Call or write for information.

*Brent Corporation*
4717 West 16 Street
Indianapolis, IN 46222
800/374-1600
317/244-6871
Fax: 317/248-9300
Service: 800/999-5456
A complete line of products for the professional potter and art education programmes. Potter's wheels, slab rollers, extruders, ware carts, Plasti-Bat, Adapta-a-Bat, Excel™ Kilns, kiln ventilation systems and other kiln supplies. Call or write for a free catalog.

*Highwater Clays*
PO Box 18284
Asheville, NC 28814
704/252-6033
High quality de-aired clays. Custom blending a speciality. In addition, they stock a full line of dry clays, glazes and glaze materials, and the finest equipment and tools available. Call or write for free catalog.

*Laguna Clay Company*
14400 East Lomitas Avenue
City of Industry, CA 91746
800/4-LAGUNA
818/330-0631
Fax: 818/333-7694
Since 1932, manufacturer and worldwide supplier of quality ceramic

equipment, tools, formulated and raw materials. High and low fire glazes and clays. Manufacturer of PACIFICA Potter's Wheels, Laguna Bonding Wheels, etc. Technical staff to answer customers' questions and solve customers' scientific and practical problems. Call for catalog and worldwide distributor information.

*Mile Hi Ceramics, Inc.*
77 Lipon
Denver, CO 80223-1580
800/456-0163
303/825-4570
Fax: 303/825-6278
Forty years in the business as one of the oldest ceramics suppliers in the U.S. Manufacturer of a complete line of pottery clays and down-draft fiber kilns. Representative for Dry Branch Kaolin. Largest distributor in the Rocky Mountain Region of materials, equipment, and supplies for the ceramist. Call or write for free catalog.

*Randall Pottery Equipment*
Box 774
Alfred, NY 14802
607/587-8655
Available wholesale or retail, the classic Randall Potter's wheel and a system of accessories and options. The heavy duty Randall extruder is always available. Brochure and price list on request.

*Seattle Pottery Supply*
Crucible Kilns
35 South Hanford
Seattle, WA 98134
800/522-1975
206/587-0570
Fax: 206/587-0373
SPS offers a complete selection of raw materials, silicon carbide and high alumina kiln shelves, ACMI-certified SPS clays and glazes and all major brands of studio equipment. Own full line of Crucible Kilns. Catalog costs $5 but includes a $5 coupon.

*Sheffield Pottery, Inc.*
Route 7 Box 399
Sheffield, MA 01257
413/229-7700
Fax: 413/229-0200
Established in 1943. Clay mined on premises for their Albany Glaze Substitute. One of the largest dry materials' inventories in the northeastern U.S. Representing Paragon kilns, Shimpo, Brent & Pacifica wheels, Kemper, Amoco, Orton, and more. Call or write for free catalog.

# FURTHER READING LIST

## Publications

*American Ceramics*
9 East 45th Street
New York, NY 10017
212/661-4397
Fax: 212/661-2389
Single copy: $7
One year: $28
Published quarterly.

*Ceramics Monthly*
Professional Publications, Inc.
P.O. Box 12448
1609 NW Blvd.
Columbus, OH 43212-0448
614/488-8236
$22/year

*Studio Potter*
Studio Potter Network Newsletter
Dept. B, Box 70
Golfstown, NH 03045
603/774-3582
Six-monthly
Subscriptions: One Year, $30

## Practical Guides

Birks, T., *The Complete Potter's Companion*. Bulfinch, Boston, Mass., 1993.
Casson, M., *The Craft of the Potter*. Barron's Educational Series, Hauppage, NY 1979.
Christy, G., *Step by Step Art School: Ceramics*. Book Sales, Seacaucus, NJ 1991.
Clark, K., *The Potter's Manual*. Book Sales, Seacaucus, NJ, 1990.
Flight, G., *Introduction to Ceramics*. Prentice-Hall, Englewood Cliffs, NJ 1990.
Fourneir, R., *Ceramic Spectrum: Clays and Glazes for the Potter*. Chiltern Publishing, PA, 1993.
Hamer, Frank, *A Potter's Dictionary of Materials and Techniques*. Watson-Guptill, New York, 1975.
Hamilton, David, *Manual of Pottery & Ceramics*. Van Nostrand Reinhold, New York, 1974.
Kenny, J. B., *The Complete Book of Pottery Making*. Chilton, Radnor, PA 1976.
Leach, B., *A Potter's Book*. Transatlantic Arts, Albuquerque, NM 1946.
Memott, Harry, *A Potter's Guide to Firing Pottery*. Deakin University, Geelong, Vic. Australia, 1993.

Sepgith, C., *Hands in Clay: Introduction to Ceramics*. Mayfield Publishing, Mountain View, CA, 1989.

The following handbooks are all published by and available from *Ceramics Monthly*:
Ball, F. C., *Decorating Pottery*.
Ballaire, M., *Underglaze Decoration*.
Behrens, R., *Ceramic Glazemaking*.
Bellaire, M., *Brush Decoration for Ceramics*.
Sellers, T. (Ed.), *Ceramic Projects*.
Sellers, T. (Ed.), *Potter's Wheel Projects*.
Sellers, T., *Throwing on the Potter's Wheel*.
Tipton, B. (Ed.), *Answers to Potter's Questions*.
Tipton, B. (Ed.), *Great Ideas for Potters*.

## Specialized areas of pottery and ceramics

Cooper, E. & Royale, D., *Glazes for the Potter*. Macmillan, Inc., New York, 1979.
Cooper, E., *The Potter's Book of Glaze*. Trafalgar Square, North Pomfret, Vermont, 1987.

## Contemporary pottery and ceramics

Garnsye, Wanda, China, *Ancient Kilns & Modern Ceramics*. A guide to the potteries, 1993.
Hopper, R., *Functional Pottery*. Chilton, Radnor, PA, 1986.
Lane, P., *Ceramic Form*. Rizzoli International, New York, NY 1988.

Nelson, G. C., *Ceramics: A Potter's Handbook*. Harcourt Brace College Publishers, Ft. Worth, Texas, 1984.
Peterson, S., *Craft and Art of Clay*. Prentice-Hall, Englewood Cliffs, NJ 1991.
Rhodes, D., *Pottery Form*. Chilton, Radnor, PA 1976.
Shaw K., *Ceramic Colours and Pottery Decoration*. Elsevier, Oxford, England 1982.

## Dictionaries

Fournier, H., *Illustrated Dictionary of Practical Pottery*. Chilton, Radnor, PA, 1992.
Hamer, F. and Hamer, J., *The Potter's Dictionary of Materials and Techniques*. Univ. of Pennsylvania Press, Philadelphia, PA 1991.

# THE AMERICAN CRAFT COUNCIL

This organization sponsors craft fairs and solicits applications for exhibitors. These juried shows are marketing events for American crafts. They draw buyers from craft galleries and shops as well as mainstream retailers, collectors, and retail customers.

American Craft Council
American Craft Enterprises
21 South Eltings Corner Road
Highland, NY 12528
800/836-3470
914/883-6100

JOHN WILHELM
*Wheel-thrown stoneware and earthenware bowl, 48 cm (18.9 in) in diameter, decorated with underglaze slip and stain and fired in an electric kiln to cone 01 (1137 °C; 2079 °F).*

# GLOSSARY

**Biscuit firing**
This is the first firing, given to greenware when it is dry and before it is glazed. The biscuit-firing temperature is lower than the temperature of the second (glaze) firing.

**Bisque firing**
A biscuit firing that is done at a higher temperature than the second (glaze or Raku) firing.

**Burnishing**
The process of polishing the surface of a pot until the clay is compacted and the surface smooth and glossy. A hard object like a smooth stone or the back of a spoon is usually used.

**Celadon**
A reduction-fired stoneware glaze, in varying shades of green-grey, depending on the amount of iron used in the glaze. Celadon glazes originated in China.

**Chun**
A Chinese stoneware glaze that fires to a pale blue in reduction. When used over an iron-bearing glaze such as a tenmoku, the blue colour is far richer and stronger. The opalescent blue colour of the glaze is caused by the way the light breaks up in the glaze and not by the addition of cobalt oxide.

**Cone**
A three-sided, pyramid-shaped object that is made of materials similar in composition to a glaze. Cones are used inside the kiln to measure the heat work and will soften and bend over when the heat work has been done and a specific temperature has been reached.

**Earthenware**
Pottery that, when fired, has a porosity of more than 5%. The maturing temperature of the clay and glazes is below 1200 °C. It is relatively soft and so, for practical use, must be glazed to make it waterproof. The clay body is available in white, buff or red.

**Frits**
An ingredient of, mainly, low-fired glazes. They are made up of glaze materials that are melted, solidified and then ground into a fine powder. Frits act as a flux in the glaze recipe (to help the glaze melt). When two materials such as lead and silica are melted together they form a lead frit, which renders the lead non-toxic and safe to use. When a soluble material is fritted it becomes insoluble when used in the glaze.

**Greenware**
These are clay pieces that have been completed but have not been fired.

**Grog**
Ground pottery or coarse sand which is added in varying percentages to the clay body. Grog helps to 'open' the clay so that it dries more evenly; it reduces the shrinkage rate of the clay during the drying and firing and therefore the tendency of clay to warp; it also provides a texture to the clay.

**Kiln**
An oven which can withstand high temperatures that is used by potters to fire pottery. There are many different types of kilns and different fuels are used to build up heat in the chamber where the pots stand.

**Leatherhard**
Clay that has dried to a stage where it is firm enough to handle, but still contains enough moisture so that knobs or handles can be joined onto it without cracking off, and so that pots can be turned. Most of the shrinkage that occurs during the drying process has occurred by the leatherhard stage.

**Oxidation**
Oxidized firings are done in electric kilns and do not change the metal oxides present in the clay and glazes so that copper gives a green colour and iron gives brown colours.

**Porcelain**
Porcelain is a high-fired, white vitreous ware with translucent qualities, depending on how thin the clay is worked. True porcelain requires a high temperature of 1300 °C (2372 °F) or more for the clay body and glaze to mature and interact. This is called a hard-paste porcelain. An imitation porcelain, or soft-paste porcelain, requires a much lower temperature for the body and glaze to mature.

**Reduction**
An atmosphere created in the kiln when firing with wood, oil or gas. Not enough oxygen is available in the kiln to complete the combustion of the flame so oxygen is taken from the metal oxides present in the pots, causing iron to turn green and copper to turn red.

**Rutile**
It comes from titanium dioxide and also has a small percentage of iron in it. When used in glazes, colours ranging from creams to oranges and yellows can be produced. The presence of rutile causes a crystallization effect which gives a broken, mottled colouring to the glaze.

**Sgraffito**
A decorating technique where a design is scratched through a layer of coloured slip, generally with a pointed tool, to reveal the contrasting colour of the clay underneath.

**Stains**
These are colouring oxides that have been stabilized and are used to colour clay and glazes.

**Stoneware**
Stoneware is a vitrified non-porous ware. The clay body and glazes are fired to about 1200 °C (2194 °F) and high-firing stoneware can be fired up to 1366 °C (2491 °F). Stoneware clay is also available in various colours — white, buff or red.

**Tenmoku**
An old Chinese stoneware reduction-fired glaze. Tenmoku glazes contain a high percentage of iron oxide (up to 10%) and are brown to black in colour and break up rust red and orange on edges and throwing rings.

## DATE DUE

| MAY 2 8 1997 | | |
|---|---|---|
| | | |
| | | |
| | | |
| | | |
| | | |
| | | |
| | | |
| | | |
| | | |
| | | |
| | | |
| | | |
| | | |
| | | |
| | | |
| | | |